CHOPIN
THE COMPOSER

CHOPIN
THE COMPOSER

HIS STRUCTURAL ART AND ITS INFLUENCE ON CONTEM-PORANEOUS MUSIC

BY

EDGAR STILLMAN KELLEY

220722

NEW YORK
COOPER SQUARE PUBLISHERS, INC.
1969

TO MY FRIEND
NAPOLEON LEDOCHOWSKI

INTRODUCTORY COMMENT

So fierce was once the conflict between the classical and romantic schools of art and literature, that the former was popularly regarded as exclusively concerned with manner and form; the latter, as dogmatically devoted to the subject-matter regardless of structural laws. In the light of subsequent research and in the calm of impartiality we find that the truly great men of the classical school possessed romantic qualities, while the masters of romanticism were keenly sensitive to the essentials of form.

In reviewing the merits of a work of art there is such a strong temptation to fall into a recounting of one's prejudices or rehearsing one's preferences that a recent writer claims that criticism is frequently merely a criticism of the opinions of others, rather than an original estimate of a given phenomenon.

Indeed, Anatole France argues that all criticism must be subjective, and the candid man can only say, "I will now talk to you about myself with reference to Shakespeare, Pascal, Voltaire, etc." If we accept this dictum, we must despair of attaining aught else than a mere personal impression of a given work. Possibly the nearest approach to a fixed criterion, or standard of objective criticism, might be obtained by means of a species of spiritual triangulation; a sort of soul-survey from different altitudes.

Various brilliant literary productions dealing with Poland's composer from a biographical, pianistic or æsthetic standpoint, have graced the tables of the music-loving world from time to time. The apology for the appearance of a treatise like the present may be found in the fact that it will not be devoted to the expression of opinions concerning the import of certain compositions and their interpretation, but rather to the discussion of that which admits of little or no dispute—the musical structure. It is to be hoped that this effort to scrutinize the subject from a point of view sufficiently divergent from the traditional, will render it of some assistance in making the trigonometrical measurement of the master's accomplishments.

Some years ago the author projected a series of essays, the object of which was to demonstrate that the music termed "romantic," as well as that which we call "classical," had its scientific justification. Among these essays may be mentioned "Classical Methods in Wagner's Music," "Tschaikowsky as a Symphonist," "Recent Developments in Musical Theory," and Sections I, XI, XIV and XV of the present work, which were published from time to time in the *Musical Courier.* The reception accorded these advance numbers of "Chopin the Composer" was such as to engender a belief that the remaining sections might also prove of interest.*

The suggestion might be made that the general reader apply himself to the beginnings and conclusions of the various sections, omitting all that appertains to the illustrations. By so doing he can rapidly seize the outline of the topics under consideration.

The writer wishes to thank the authorities of The Western College for providing him with the leisure and quiet requisite for the elaboration of the present work and making it possible for him to undertake other long-cherished projects.

He would also express his indebtedness to the Editor of "The Musical Observer" for the rare portrait of Chopin, which forms the frontispiece of the book.

---

*Much of this material has been remodelled from lectures delivered during several seasons at Albany (State University Extension), also from others prepared for Columbia and Yale Universities.

CONTENTS

CHOPIN
THE COMPOSER

PRELUDIUM

Those men of genius who cannot be surpassed may be equalled.
How? By being different.*   *Victor Hugo.*

The musical world is now passing through a wonderful constellation of centennials. So numerous was the group of heroes born in or about the year 1810, that the celebrations in honor of these immortals follow each other with almost unseemly rapidity. Flippant writers are even disposed to be facetious. Never mind! The journalists in the latter end of our century will not be thus overburdened. There will be less crowding then.

What occasioned this congestion? Was it the result of mere chance? By no means. What, then, was it?

On reviewing the epoch-making events of the eighteenth century, we find a condition of affairs startling in its abnormity. The successful efforts of those high in authority to monopolize power had, after ages of accretion, come to such a focus of absolutism that oppressed humanity could no longer endure the strain. Then followed the inevitable reaction in the effort to readjust matters. Phases of this reaction are known as the French Revolution, the Reign of Terror, and the Napoleonic Wars. During those awful upheavals were brought forth ideas of such magnitude, griefs so keen, and passions so tempestuous, that words alone were inadequate to express them. Music, therefore, the most emotional of all the arts, was called upon to act as interpreter. But this interpreter was not to be the bland, placid music of the rococo school. There existed latent in the language of tone possibilities far greater than were apprehended by the *ancien régime*. Indeed, the world had waited many centuries for

---

*Obviously, Victor Hugo, in making this statement, did not dream of implying that mere "difference" was a merit. His conception of the term "difference" refers to another phase of beauty and intellectuality.

the revelation of this richer expression. But who was to awaken these slumbering powers?

Men yet unborn. Therefore it was, that the unprecedented occurred.

Never in the history of music has there appeared such a group of stars of the first magnitude in such close proximity as when the Romanticists made their advent. True, Bach and Händel immortalized the year 1685. But, clustering about the date 1810, we see Hector Berlioz, born in 1803; Mendelssohn in 1809; Chopin and Schumann in 1810; Liszt in 1811; Wagner and Verdi in 1813; and Robert Franz in 1815. Furthermore, these are hard pressed by numerous stars of the second magnitude, such as Nicolai, Félicien and Ferdinand David, 1810; F. Hiller and Ambroise Thomas, 1811; and Henselt, 1814. If we include in this series Schubert, who was more modern in his sympathies than Mendelssohn, we find that these dates outline the stormiest period of Napoleon's career. The oldest, Franz Schubert (1797), first saw light two weeks after the battle of Rivoli; the last, Robert Franz, ten days after the battle of Waterloo.

On listening to the music most characteristic of these illustrious men, we perceive numerous features previously unknown. Richer harmonies are employed, sharper dissonances are introduced, more rapid modulations are indulged in, unique rhythms devised; on the whole effecting a more direct and immediate emotional appeal. All this impels us to acknowledge that Nature had thus provided an ideal means of voicing not only the grief and despair, but the longing and hope of mankind, and in so doing gave the world a new and powerful school of art. This constellation, therefore, was not the result of blind fortuity, but of Divine forethought.

The scholarly Griepenkerl, in his edition of Bach's organ works, calls attention to the fact that the highly praised compositions of Palestrina, based as they are so largely on triads, contain too little incentive to progression. Bach, by employing more complex material, including dissonances that compel a movement to a satisfying consonance, introduced a valuable æsthetic element which entitles him to a higher rank than Palestrina.* Similarly it may be said that, with all respect and reverence for the classical symphonists, the romantic writers enriched many phases of music. Indeed, various procedures peculiar to them are virtually the elaborations of principles already applied by Bach. Again, we note certain phenomena with which the Leipzig cantor was absolutely unfamiliar, but of which he would have emphatically approved, inasmuch as they represent æsthetically justifiable processes logically followed to satisfactory results.

Among the strongest individualities in the romantic constellation stands a bold youth from the country that produced Kopernik. And as Copernicus, by virtue of his astronomical discoveries, stimulated the great Kepler to perfect his revolutionary theories, so, too, has this Polish composer exerted an influence on creative minds outside the boundaries of his native land. The originality and charm of his music are generally admitted, and early secured him a world-wide reputation. But, as Theodore Roosevelt says, "Scientific accuracy and literary charm are two qualities generally deemed (by certain scholars) as mutually inconsistent." The power of this deplorable superstition is also manifest in the musical world; consequently, the beauty and originality which vitalize the works of the great Pole are supposed by many to preclude those intellectual qualities without which none can lay claim to true artistic greatness. Thus it follows that certain critics have felt it incumbent upon them so to emphasize the defects—real or assumed—in Chopin's writings that the uninitiated are frequently led to regard him as an amateur rather than a master.

---

*Bach, J. S., Organ Works. Edited by F. C. Griepenkerl; Peters Edition, Vol. III (No. 242).

Only three or four decades had passed over the grave of Beethoven when theorists like Marx and Richter justified, in their text-books, the application of the master's discoveries. Sixty years have now elapsed since the death of the great Polish composer, and it seems as though the time were ripe for investigating such of his structural innovations as have proved profitable to subsequent artists.

I
NEED FOR A REVALUATION

Chopin is the great inspired tone-poet who properly should be named only with Mozart, Beethoven and Rossini. *Heinrich Heine.*

In making an analysis of Chopin we meet with beauties of a high order, expressions entirely new, and a harmonic tissue as original as it is erudite. . . . Oh! we have not yet studied with sufficient earnestness and attention the designs of his delicate pencil. . . . . His best works abound in combinations which may be said to mark an epoch in the formation of style. . . . Their worth has, however, already been felt; but it will be more highly estimated when the time arrives for a critical examination. *Franz Liszt.*

Chopin the pianist, Chopin the tone-poet, Chopin the heartbroken patriot, Chopin the disconsolate lover, Chopin the invalid, the morbid, even the decadent artist, has been discussed, exploited, admired, adored, reviled and rejected according to the mental, moral and emotional conditions of those who have considered the merits of the great Pole whose centennial was recently celebrated. But, singularly enough, Chopin the composer is still something of an unknown quantity. So strikingly unconventional are his works, so spontaneous his themes, so startling his rhythmic and harmonic devices, that nothing but their great beauty has induced the severe contrapuntists to give him any sort of serious consideration.

Among the first to write concerning the position Chopin deserves to take among the world's great composers, was his devoted friend Liszt, whose biography is obviously a labor of love. In the introductory chapter he says: "If it were our intention to discuss the development of piano music in the language of the schools, we should dissect his magnificent pages, which afford so rich a field for scientific observation." It may be seen from this, that Liszt divined something of the high intellectuality which permeates all Chopin's work; but so fascinating is his thematic material, so exciting its emotional quality, and so artistically has the artist concealed his art, that thousands of his devotees are firmly convinced that the enchantment which translates one from the every-day world to an ideal realm, is due to a spell woven by genius unassisted by culture. It is deeply to be deplored that Liszt did not give us an insight into the mysteries of Chopin's architectural art. The lack of it has been a loss to musical science. Liszt might at least have dwelt at greater length on Chopin's theoretical training and more firmly insisted on his technical acquirements, which rendered him, at so early an age, a fully equipped composer.* But, unfortunately, the biographer maintains that "This is not the time or place for such a study, which would be interesting only to adepts in counterpoint and thorough-bass." So great was Liszt's enthusiasm for the rich contributions to musical literature left by the Polish composer, that he made it his mission to proclaim to the world their poetical and spiritual import. So strongly did this self-imposed duty weigh upon him, that he expressed his feelings in a panegyric of such dithyrambic character, that the few words concerning his friend's creative skill are overlooked and forgotten. To make matters worse we are told in so many words that Chopin "was one of those original beings whose graces are fully displayed only when they have cut themselves adrift from all bondage, and float on at their own wild will, swayed wholly by the ever undulating impulses of

---

*Chopin's teacher, Joseph Elsner, was a prolific and versatile composer whose operas, oratorios, orchestral works, etc., were held in esteem even beyond the boundaries of Poland. So easy is it for a young artist to be led astray by foolishly indulgent pedagogues, or to lose his individuality through overbearing pedantry, that the world is under especial obligations to Elsner. His refined taste, wholesome nature, thorough scholarship and conscientious artistic guidance, were invaluable to one of Chopin's hypersensitive, overmodest, easily discouraged disposition. Elsner's generous solicitude for the normal development of the creative gifts of his unusual pupil is amply evidenced by the monitory epistles to the latter, quoted by Karasowski.

their own mobile natures." This reference to the "wild will" has undoubtedly given a coloring to Liszt's monograph that is misleading to the reader, be he professional or amateur. When such a stand was taken by one of Chopin's best friends and most intelligent admirers, one whose keen, critical discernment and warm sympathies rendered him the most far-sighted musical prophet the world has ever known, it was but natural for others, less gifted, to assume a similar attitude. Professor Niecks, in his statistically excellent and fairly sympathetic life of Chopin, goes so far as to criticize Liszt for employing the word *scientific* in connection with this artist, implying that there is little to be found in his compositions worthy of so dignified a term. The learned writer, like many others, evidently associates the word scientific only with counterpoint, canon, fugue, and their cognates; hence, compositions in which these elements are not immediately obvious must needs be *un*scientific. But there are various methods of constructing and decorating musical edifices, all demanding the application of scientific principles, and it is due to their scientific structure that Chopin's creations have survived the storms of criticism and the erosions of time.

After studying the Chopinesque architecture, one is able to demonstrate what so many have long felt, but few have dared to say; namely, that it is as absurd to criticize Chopin for not writing sonatas in the style of Beethoven as it would be to belittle the latter for not composing fugues after the manner of Bach.

Some authors contemplate the Pole's marvelous creations from the pathological standpoint, regarding them as phenomena whose nature and origin are akin to that of those pearls whose very existence is due to some injury done to the passive mollusk. This view, however, despite the high value placed on the ultimate product, detracts materially from the merits of an artist, alike great in powers of invention and in the conscientious exercise of the same.

Not many months since, while interchanging views with one of Germany's ablest composers, a man of fine feeling and breadth of vision, I touched on Chopin's special gifts in construction. My friend was most enthusiastic about the quality of the work, but to my surprise mentioned the old familiar criticisms about weakness in sonata-form, orchestration, etc. He furthermore observed, semi-humorously, that "in the eyes of a great contrapuntist like Kiel, Chopin would not have been regarded as a musician" (*er hätte nicht als Musiker gegolten*). Another friend, a great virtuoso, spoke of Chopin in one breath as the greatest composer for the piano, and in the next he added, "but, of course, he was no musician like Brahms." The summer of 1908 I spent in Eisenach, where I saw a good deal of the venerable composer Carl Reinecke. On one occasion he did me the honor of reading portions of an article he was then preparing for some literary journal, on Mendelssohn and Chopin, apropos of the approaching centennial.

His unaffected admiration for both was truly refreshing in this blasé age. He expressed great appreciation for the Polish genius, "whose works possess an unaccountable charm for the laity, as well as for members of the guild, but whose genius it is impossible to classify!"

How strange that, from standpoints so diverse, much the same verdict is rendered with respect to this unique artist. One class of musicians refuses to admit Chopin to the inner circle because he does not express himself in terms of *cantus firmus, punctus contra punctum, dux et comes;* while another group, equally numerous, deems it desecration to apply square, compass and plumb-line to his structures, as we would to those of one of the classical architects. The fact that the works of Chopin have not only survived to the present day, but are more universally known, studied and played than ever before, shows that they must possess vitality. This implies that they contain something besides mere sensuous charm, which soon palls if devoid of intellectual qualifications; and it is to the intellectual side of Chopin's work that our attention shall be directed.

Although early imbued with a feeling of awe and reverence for the classical masters, it was not until undertaking the serious study of music that I became familiar with the curious name, Chopin. So strangely beautiful was everything connected with this name, that I searched all possible sources of information concerning its possessor, finding at length the "Life" by Liszt. The bewildering phraseology of poetry, music, art and love, left the impression that Chopin was a man of unusual genius, who knew naught of art's laws—nor did he need them, so great were his inherent powers. When, in the Western metropolis, I began the ordeal of counterpoint under the sympathetic guidance of Clarence Eddy, then fresh from his first Berlin successes, I one day bewailed the fact that I was not a genius like Chopin, who wrote such wonderful things without bothering about theory. Whereupon, to my great surprise, I was told that "Chopin studied counterpoint assiduously, and in his piano work devoted himself seriously to Bach."

Another shock soon came. My piano-teacher was Napoleon Ledochowski, a gentleman whose family belonged to the Polish nobility, and who for some decades had found a congenial home in Paris.* I was, of course, greatly interested to learn that the Chopin and Ledochowski families had long been intimate. Among the students in the academy of Pro-

---

*This family, too, has experienced the "historic sorrow of the Pole," leading for the most part lives in foreign lands. The grandfather of my instructor was an officer in the army of Napoleon I; while his brother played a prominent part in the defense of Warsaw in 1831, the father, together with other kinsmen, escaped to France, joining the army of the latter country. Another distinguished member of this family was the late Cardinal Ledochowski, private secretary of Leo XIII.

fessor Nicolas Chopin was the grandfather of my teacher,*
and at the betrothal of his parents Chopin the composer
played.

As was but natural, I sought to learn all that I could from
so authoritative a source concerning the Polish composer and
his works, and one day expressed my admiration for Chopin's
freedom from rule-observance. Like all young students, I
felt that one of the chief requisites in creating works of pronounced originality was to break all known rules. I have
never forgotten Ledochowski's reply: "It may seem so to
you now, but after you have studied the laws of form and
composition, you will find that although they are much more
complex, the works of Chopin are based upon the same fundamental principles as those of Mozart and Beethoven, and
you will find them equally susceptible of analysis."

Later, while continuing my studies in Germany, I hoped
to learn something definite about Chopin's workmanship; but
aside from conventional comments on his beautiful melodies,
harmonies, modulations, etc., with here and there a word
about a stray indiscretion concerning the simplest progressions, I recall nothing positive relating to his theoretical attainments, excepting a casual mention by a fellow-student of
the bit of imitation which he found in the introduction of the
A♭ Ballade. When, therefore, I saw the Kullak edition and
read the bold assertion that the motto in the great *A*-minor
Étude Op. 25, No. 11, is worthy to rank with the incisive
initial motive of Beethoven's *C*-minor Symphony, and that
the elaboration is worthy of the theme, I rejoiced to find
some one in authority who shared Ledochowski's views. The
pronounced claims in behalf of Chopin's genius made by
Langhans in his "History of Music," Henry T. Finck's bril-

---

*Having been reared among the Franco-Polish aristocracy (his mother
being a daughter of Baron Maneval, secretary of Napoleon I), he enjoyed
rare opportunities of absorbing the Chopin traditions directly from the
master's pupils.

liant and daring lecture (since published), and the historic
Chopin recitals of de Pachmann, were, to me, great incentives
to deeper investigation into the mystico-mathematical problems presented by the Chopinesque architecture.

More recently, Huneker continually and unhesitatingly
places Chopin among the group of the greatest—Bach, Beethoven, Wagner—justly stating that he had as great harmonic genius as Wagner and greater melodic gifts; in the
flow of his melody being equalled only by Schubert.

I fully believe that we are justified in making the statement
that all music with rich harmonic texture, composed since the
thirties and forties of the last century, shows Chopin's influence either directly or indirectly. Tschaikowsky, it is
true, for political reasons did not like the great Pole. Still,
his fondness for Schumann is almost everywhere evident, and
the latter, as we all know, was in intimate sympathy with
Chopin. To say nothing of how his works have affected
subsequent composers, it would be interesting to learn what
Mozart would have said to a passage like this:

EXAMPLE 1

What a thrilling surprise after the *stretto, forte,* and the hold!
Mozart and Beethoven (likewise Mendelssohn, and even

Schubert) would have continued with a chord of the sixth and fourth, as at Example 1b. How uninteresting this sounds to us who are familiar with Chopin's version, which is neither preposterous nor *outré*. (See Example 1a.)   He merely employs the minor subdominant triad in the first inversion— but, following as it does the first inversion of the triad on the second degree, we have a chord-progression as beautiful as it is unprecedented.

What would Beethoven have thought of the unexpected change, so gracefully effected, from C major into E major in the $E\flat$-minor Étude Op. 10, No. 6?

EXAMPLE 2

How would Bach have been impressed by the harmonic outline of the F-major Étude Op. 25, No. 3? The second part modulates into B major, the most distant of tonalities, whence, in a similar series of transitions, it returns to the main key with the utmost freedom and naturalness.*

---

*It is indeed singular that so gifted a composer and so enthusiastic a critic as Schumann should have overlooked this most original scheme of modulation. But he passed it by with the simple comment that this étude is less interesting than the preceding one (in F minor), referring merely to the technical figures. Here we have a striking instance of the necessity of inspecting Chopin's works scientifically, if we are fully to appreciate their structural beauties. (See the analysis of this étude in Section VI.)

These examples, chosen almost at random, serve to show that Chopin seems to have apprehended, as had none of his predecessors, the hidden relationship existing between far-away keys; and again, that he could impart to those more closely akin a mystic semblance of distance, when occasion required. The study of his works from this point alone is of the greatest value in enabling one to avoid meaningless repetitions and aimless wanderings into foreign keys, whence there is no hope of return in time to save the tonality.

How many young composers, often with good themes at command, find themselves floundering about in a tempestuous sea of sound with neither compass nor anchor, merely because they have had no training other than the conventional classical. If they will confine themselves to the classical *themata* and modulatory outlines, well and good. But if they wish to address themselves to the solution of more recent problems, such as the harmonic design and the modulating theme, they should add to their study of Bach and Beethoven, for fugue and development, the careful study of Chopin's methods of construction.

Realizing how severely the great masters now suffer from over-editing—Chopin possibly most of all—the foregoing comment is not made without some hesitation, for it might easily incite the overzealous to ruthless dissections of ideal creations, or to hair-splitting analyses of Chopin's subtle chord-formations. But is it not possible to show enough of Chopin's art to reveal new and unexpected beauties, without reducing his system to a *Schablone,* a stencil-pattern, to be employed *ad nauseam?* Only a few of the principal features can be touched upon, but as these are of vital importance it is to be hoped that this suggestive, rather than exhaustive method of presenting the evidence, may lead to individual investigation on the lines indicated.

II

NATIONAL ELEMENTS

The latent and unknown poetry, which was only indicated in the original Polish Mazurkas, was divined, developed and brought to light by Chopin. Preserving their rhythm, he ennobled their melody, enlarged their proportions, and wrought into their tissues harmonic lights and shadows, as new in themselves as were the subjects to which he adapted them. *Franz Liszt.*

All who are acquainted with the career of Chopin are aware that his works are imbued with a spirit of devotion to his native land, and that in many of them distinctive local color is obvious. The very titles of two of his volumes, "Mazurkas" and "Polonaises," proclaim their Sarmatian origin. Nevertheless, to what extent the composer employed native material and in how far he has permitted his imagination to be influenced by genuinely popular airs, few concern themselves. Professor Niecks gives, I believe, the first definite information with regard to this national material. He relates in a charming manner how Chopin visited the rural districts and took great pains to write down those songs and dances that grew up among the people. This collection formed the fund of folk-music upon which he drew in later years for the characteristic features of his works.

Let us devote ourselves briefly to a consideration of what constitutes such characteristics; let us think ourselves back some seventy years, and fancy ourselves living in London or Paris, accustomed only to the music of Western Europe. This music, be it remembered, was composed almost exclusively in the major or minor keys; the rhythms were for the most part simple, and the accents strongly marked at the beginning of each measure. Let us try to imagine how a mazurka of Chopin would impress the average layman whose life had been spent in this musical environment.

14

At first he would probably realize that the melody possessed peculiar traits; then, that the rhythms were quite out of the ordinary; lastly, he would be conscious of harmonies quite new to him. Repeated hearings would show, very likely, that the melody could not be played within the confines of a given major or minor key (which usually satisfies the peoples of Western Europe), and that this, too, necessarily affected the harmony. The reason of this peculiarity is, that many of the folk-songs and dances which Chopin utilized and idealized were conceived in the church modes, as is often the case with Russian and other Slavic national airs.

Let the student who has not occupied himself especially with these modes, play over the formula in Example 3a on the different degrees of the *C*-major scale, touching neither *sharps* nor *flats*.

EXAMPLE 3

The scales thus formed will give us the different ecclesiastical modes, namely, *C* to *C*, Ionian; *D* to *D*, Dorian; *E* to *E*, Phrygian; *F* to *F*, Lydian; *G* to *G*, Mixolydian; *A* to *A*, Æolian. The peculiarities of the different modes may be still more firmly impressed upon the mind by adding to each the appropriate transposition of the cadence-formula shown in Example 3b. Such formulas, though rarely employed in the harmonization of these modes, may be permitted here by way of illustration, as they bring out, more clearly than the simple tone-series, the deviations of the respective modes from our major and minor scales. Compare those based upon the Lydian and Mixolydian with that of the Ionian mode, or the major scale.

When we listen to the Arabs, on the Midway Plaisance, rendering one of our street melodies we are amused (if we recognize it at all) at the alterations introduced to suit their taste.   But we must not forget that, conversely, when our musicians make use of an exotic melody (that is, a melody not conceived in one of our major or minor keys) it is "adapted" to render it intelligible to our public.   I once heard a Polish street musician play a popular air on his hurdy-gurdy. (See Example 4a.)   Unless the listener were on the lookout for such curios, he would not realize that by changing one note (*F* to *F*♯) he would throw it from the original mode (Mixolydian, or *G* major with *F*♮) into our conventional major, and then we should have the commonplace "Cracovienne" as we know it.   (See Example 4b, comparing N. B. 1 with N. B. 2.)

EXAMPLE 4

How vast is the difference between such a cheapening of these native products and Chopin's "ennobling" of the same, to which Liszt refers.   Those who are familiar with Niecks's "Life of Chopin," will recall the interesting group of Polish airs therein given.   One observes occasional intervallic and rhythmic peculiarities, but rarely, if ever, finds anything that reminds him of the refinements of the master.   It is the mission of Genius to beautify. If we examine certain of the mazurkas, we shall discover, not necessarily traces of the original airs (for we have no means of knowing what melodies inspired this or that number), but we can learn something of the modes, or keys, which lend them their peculiar tints.

In the Mazurka Op. 24, No. 2, we find suggestions of no less than three of these modes. The first period gives the impression of Æolian (minor with minor dominant). Note with what care Chopin avoids the third in the dominant seventh-chord in the fourth measure of Example 5a. G♮ in connection with the seventh would sound out of place, while G♯ would destroy the Æolian quality of the phrase.

EXAMPLE 5

The second period has a flavor of Dorian (minor, with major triads on the fourth and seventh degrees). This juxtaposition of the major triad on the seventh degree (*C*) with the minor triad on the first (*D*) we find in certain ancient Scotch airs, such as "Queen Mary's Escape from Loch Leven Castle." In the above instance, the tragic beauty of this mode is softened by the interposed *C* major dominant seventh-chord, which for an instant changes its character, giving a suggestion (possibly) of the Hypomixolydian.

But we must not forget that it is possible to pass from a
mode to a minor or major key, the same as we change a major
theme into a minor, and *vice versa*. A magnificent illustration of throwing a major motive into the Mixolydian may be
found in the last measures of the last movement of Grieg's
A-minor Concerto. Here, while the pianist performs a long
scale-passage, the orchestra gives utterance to the second
theme *fortissimo;* but the first note of the first triplet is *G*♮
instead of *G*♯.*

Example 6, from the third period of the Mazurka above
quoted, affords an excellent illustration of the Lydian
(*F* major with *B*♮).

EXAMPLE 6

This mode, with its quaint, eccentric qualities, is much less
frequently used than the others, although Chopin touches
upon it several times in his mazurkas. The harmonic outline of Example 6 appears four times in succession, twice
without the peculiar feature at N. B. and twice with it, in
which case it is marked *ritenuto,* that we may enjoy the
subtle flavor of the Lydian mode.†

There remains one more mode, the Phrygian, to be illustrated, and in this connection I should like to give its ancient

---

*Grieg, in a happy, exuberant letter to his parents, dated Rome, April,
1870, relates how Liszt showed his enthusiasm on playing through this work
for the first time.—"Stretching out his arms in an imperial manner, he called
out, 'G natural, G natural, *not* G sharp!'" ("Edvard Grieg," a Biography
by Schjelderup; C. F. Peters, Leipzig.)

†See also the Mazurka, Op. 68, No. 3, for another specimen of Lydian.
In the *Poco più vivo,* we have the key of *B*♭ with *E*♮.

prototype, the Greek Dorian scale. It will be noticed that
the latter *descends* and has a downward leading-tone, as in
Example 7a at N. B., whereas the former (the Phrygian)
ascends, and the whole step between the seventh and eighth
degrees calls for a cadence which produces the impression of a
close in the dominant of the minor scale. (See Example 7b.)
The opening measures of the Mazurka Op. 41, No. 1, is
Phrygian in feeling, although it does not contain the cadence
characteristic of that mode. (See Example 7c, transposed
for convenience.)

EXAMPLE 7

The Greek Dorian is beautifully illustrated in Chopin's
Tarentelle, Op. 43. (See Example 7d.) To show one of
the thousand devices at the command of the ever-ready artist,
which enabled him to lend new beauty to old material, glance
at his version of the Phrygian close from the B♭-minor
Scherzo. (See Example 7e.) Compare the progression at
7f with the conventional close at 7g, and note the surprising
transformation.

It will be remembered that while Poland was an independent kingdom, it formed a buffer-state. That its close

proximity to Turkey should to some extent affect the character of the people, their customs, their mode of thought and art-expression, was but natural. This accounts for numerous passages in Chopin which indicate Moslem influence.

The fondness of the Orientals for the step of the augmented second is well known.* Indeed, Helmholtz believed that the leading-tone in the minor scale was brought westward by the crusaders. Bearing this in mind, the student, on playing the last strain in the Mazurka Op. 7, No. 1, will realize that it was not a mere whim on the part of the composer, or an arbitrary effort to insert something queer. (See Example 8a.)

EXAMPLE 8

Another familiar suggestion of this tonality may be seen in Op. 68, No. 2 (see Example 8b). Careful inspection will reveal the fact that this theme is not conceived in the key of

*Of course, in the Arabian and Persian systems this interval is only approximate.

A minor, neither can we regard it as being in *E* minor. It involves the use of the tones given in series c and d of Example 8, which indicate Asiatic rather than European origin. Liszt, in his monograph on Chopin, dwells at some length on the social customs and temperamental traits derived by the Poles from their Musselmanic neighbors, but strangely enough makes no mention of the music of the latter. So strongly tinged with Orientalism are certain themes employed by Chopin, that a well-known English writer maintains that "the composer's enforced sojourn in Paris exerted a salutary influence on his art, inasmuch as it toned down his Arabian howl."

But the music of the Poles was also strongly influenced by the Moslems in other respects, especially with regard to rhythm. Those who have listened to the music of the Orientals, or observed the clog-dances of the negroes, will have noticed the singular fondness of these peoples for complex rhythms, and the tendency to place the strong accents "off the beat." This fact was emphasized by Professor Stumpf of the University of Berlin in a recent lecture before the *Internationale Musik-Gesellschaft* on "The Beginnings of Music." According to this eminent authority, the origin of our art was rhythmic, and as horizontal music (rhythmic) is the enemy of the vertical (harmonic), the lovers of the one do not understand that of the other. Hence, Europeans accustomed to the vertical lose many interesting features of the horizontal music. Substantiation of this statement was afforded us by means of phonographic records of primitive folk-music, also by songs of a South African negro, with hand-drum accompaniment so rhythmically complex that it was amusingly elusive.

Bearing all this in mind, it is not difficult to believe that the Orient is largely accountable for the passion of the Poles, and other Slavs, for placing the strongest stress on the second and third beats of the measure in their mazurkas and other

dances.   Comment has been made on the preference of ama-
teurs for Chopin's waltzes.   This is simply because the people
of Western Europe content themselves with heavy beats on
the first of the measure, whereas the mazurkas contain many
syncopations and other rhythmic intricacies which render
them difficult of performance.   But the question may be asked,
"How can a dancer express any rhythm, aside from the heavy
and light beats in a measure, containing only two or three
steps?"   This would, indeed, be impossible were the feet
clad in ordinary shoes or boots, but the Polish country-people
wear pattens or clogs in dancing, which enable them to execute (or rattle) a great variety of complicated rhythmic figures.*   Those who have ever observed the clog-dancing of
our American negro minstrels, or that of the *Schuhplättler* of
the Bavarian Alps, will appreciate the fact that figures of
great complexity can be produced by skillful control of heel
and toe.   When Chopin made his collection of folk-melodies
it included many rhythmic features derived from this humble
source, but of great value, as may be seen from the very first
mazurka that appeared from his pen.   (See Example 9, from
Op. 6, No. 1.)   It is easy to imagine this beautiful dance
executed rhythmically, *i. e.,* without a single note of music.

That Chopin's music was predestined to bear the stamp of
harmonic distinction, one can readily apprehend from the curious curves taken by the melodies, especially those sprinkled
with chromatic tones, as in the familiar piece quoted in Ex. 9.
Observe the symmetry of the structure, how the harmonic
outline corresponds with the rhythmic in the first two measures, with chords of the dominant seventh and tonic in the
main key ($F\sharp$ minor), followed by a sequence in the relative
major.   The fifth measure presents us with a bold yet plau-
sible harmonization of the tones $C\sharp$, $B\sharp$, $B\natural$.   The sixth and
seventh measures are exact sequences; the eighth, another

---

*Czerwinski's "Brevier der Tanzkunst: Die Tänze bei den Kultur-Völ-
kern," Leipzig, 1881.

slightly varied, so that we are led back to the tonic again.
Note the logical development of each feature; the suspension
with which the movement opens being preserved throughout,
at all vital points (1st, 3d, 5th, 6th, 7th, 8th). This little piece
contains numerous elements of Chopin's greatness, and is well

EXAMPLE 9

worth careful inspection, not only on account of its *"volks-
thümlich"* character, but by virtue of its rhythmic, melodic
and harmonic development.

But we must not forget, when all is said and done, that, as
in English literature the most forceful style reveals the greatest percentage of Anglo-Saxon, so likewise, in music, the most
powerful is indicated by a goodly proportion of diatonic passages sustained by triads. We find, accordingly, that with all
his rich fund of new material at command, one great source
of Chopin's strength was his capacity for devoting himself

whole-heartedly to diatonic melodies and fundamental harmonies. His personal attachment to Bellini and admiration for his *bel canto* is well known.* Sometimes, as in the Trio of the Polonaise Op. 40, No. 1, we have a theme as elemental as a bugle-call. Wagner, who was grandly diatonic at times, employed equally primitive motives, and with signal success; witness the Sword theme and the Rhinegold fanfare in the Trilogy. It is only by employing the appropriate means for the expression of the infinite variety of emotions experienced by the Genius, that the true proportions of a work of art can be maintained. Helmholtz, as early as 1862, expressed his convictions concerning the desirability of maintaining the proper balance between consonances and dissonances. "In many modern compositions dissonant chords form the majority and consonant chords the minority, yet no one can doubt that this is the reverse of what ought to be the case; and continual bold modulational leaps threaten entirely to destroy the feeling for tonality. These are unpleasant symptoms for the further development of art." The later Wagnerian works seem to emphasize with ever-increasing stress the truth of what Helmholtz says above, not only concerning the advantages and beauties of modulation, but also with regard to the evils arising from the loss of sense of tonality resulting from too many foreign harmonies. In behalf of Chopin's music, and the greater portion of Wagner's, it must be stated that what in many instances seem to be so many dissonances are, strictly speaking, highly decorated triads and primary seventh-chords. Not until we reach the post-Nibelungian period of music, do we find such quantities of vague tonality, that the prophecy of Helmholtz comes to us like a warning of the approaching end—a possible *Kunst-Dämmerung*.

---

*At his own request, it is said, Chopin was buried beside Bellini in the cemetery of Père La Chaise.

III

THE EXPONENT OF THE IMPROVED PIANO-FORTE

Chopin's fancy was inexhaustible in the discovery of new kinds of scattered chords, combined into harmony by his novel use of the pedal; in this way he so enriched music that he must be placed, as a harmonic innovator, on a level with Bach and Wagner.

Henry T. Finck.

Every age has its possibilities and its limitations. This is true, not only of the material conditions, but also of the current thought and the means of giving it utterance, whether in Art or in Literature. From the days of Cristofori the instruments with keys (harpsichords, clavichords, etc.) had been gradually growing in technical perfection until Bach, by employing the equal temperament, made modulation possible. His Well-Tempered Clavichord marks an era to be remembered with the utmost gratitude. Another century passed, and the pianoforte had so gained in compass and strength, that the writing and performance of Beethoven's sonatas were attendant features. Other improvements followed, and the favorite household instrument acquired still greater size and power. Moreover, new effects were made feasible by means of the improved damper-pedal, which suggested the art of refined shading and the development of overtones hitherto lost. This was bound to bring about a change of style.

Whereas the lack of sonority in the old instruments had rendered it imperative to write all chords to be played with one hand in close position (within the compass of an octave), it now became not only practicable, but desirable, to distribute them. We already find in Weber's music attempts at wider dispersion. Chopin, with true scientific intuition, realized that by following the suggestive outline of the Nature-Scale a

more sonorous and refined disposition of his harmonies could
be effected than by means of the old method.*

EXAMPLE 10

By comparing the various extracts given in Example 11
(from his Rondo Op. 1) it will be noticed that he applied
this scheme from the outset.   The passages at a and b might
have been written by Mozart or Beethoven; at c and d, however, we have something quite new.

EXAMPLE 11

*Others had experimented with little jumps of tenths. Weber, in the trio
of "Invitation to the Dance"; Beethoven, Trio Op. 1, No. 1, Finale, and
Sonata Op. 2, No. 3, first movement, third measure. (Here, indeed, we find
a tenth struck and held.)   Later Hummel and Field used them more frequently.

As the visitor stands in the choir of Winchester Cathedral, his attention is called to those portions of the structure which retain the round arches of the Norman and then to those re-modeled by William of Wykeham into the pointed arches of the Perpendicular style.* The figure shown in Example 11c presents a similar turning-point in the history of piano music. Note the grouping of the tones in the bass; there are no thirds as at a, but all are more in accord with the diagram given in Example 10. A striking illustration of this method is afforded by the Prelude in E♭. Here Finck's happy expression "scattered chords" may be fittingly applied. (See Example 12.)

EXAMPLE 12

With the rich fund of National material at his command, and a new instrument inviting him to a fertile field of discovery, one's curiosity is piqued to learn something of the theoretical attainments Chopin would be likely to display. His training, under a skillful teacher and composer, has been mentioned, also his predilection for Bach.

A recently published work concerning the career of George Sand, by Francis Gribble, contains a significant quotation

---

*The Early English and Decorated styles had indeed intervened, but rarely do we find such a clear-cut transition from one mode of art-expression to another as is here instanced. Chronologically speaking, the adoption by the gifted bishop of the Norman style as a starting-point for a new type of architecture, is paralleled by the procedure of the Romantic music-masters who derived their precedent from Bach, rather than from the great symphonists.

from one of Chopin's letters written during his sojourn in the old cloister on the island of Majorca.

"My cell is about as large as a coffin, a vault thick with dust serving as a lid. The windows are small, and underneath these windows grow orange-trees, palms, and cypresses. Opposite to them, underneath a rose window in the Arabian style, is my bed. Close to the bed is a small table; and on this table—a great luxury—stand a metal candlestick, holding a miserable candle, the works of Bach, and my own compositions in manuscript. That is the full list of my belongings. And what a silence!"

This silence (which, Chopin adds, was so profound that one might shout at the top of his voice without awakening a response) afforded a rare background for the setting of Bach's tone-creations. It is easy to see that this singular preference shown the Leipzig cantor by the young Pole was genuine and inevitable. Such devotion had nothing in common with that amateurish adoration for everything by Bach, even the most prosaic, so long as it savors of wig and wax candles. This unusual combination of natural beauties, romantic surroundings, and exalted musical stimulus, could not fail to produce its effect on so impressionable a being as Chopin. Indeed, the Bach influence had long since manifested itself.

Take the first Étude of the Op. 10 group. What bold sweeps throughout the entire range of the new pianoforte! It seems as though the spirit of Bach had appeared to the young Pole and dictated a magnified Preludium, with wider reaches and broader scope than was possible, even for the elder master, who had only the four-octave clavichord at his command. Note the beautiful distribution of the chords, and the weaving back and forth of the voices.* It is of the ut-

---

*It seems as though everything had conspired to render the young composer peculiarly qualified to create a new pianoforte school. Even the mechanical appliance he had invented to stretch his pliant fingers and give them greater capacity for extension, stood him in good stead. Witness the appalling chord-dispersions throughout this étude, distances which no one till then had dreamed of reaching.

most importance to bear this Bach influence constantly in mind, as it furnishes the only clue to the mysteries presented by so many of those passages which charm us, we scarce know why at first; but which, on tracing their outlines with care, discover that what with so many writers would be mere padding, is with Chopin a finely conceived series of *inner*-voice progressions. Example 12 shows how the peculiar zig-zagging of the apparently two-part movement will furnish material for six distinct parts.

If all parts are played simultaneously, a passage of singular richness results. Octaves will occur in the first measure, between the third and sixth voices, it is true, but these are easily avoided by giving *B* natural instead of *D* to the bass (voice 6) on the second beat. But how much less sonorous is this third in the bass! Observe the master's care in the matter of dispersion, and it is evident that the outlines formed by voices 1, 2, 5 and 6 are the main objects in view. More than this, it was a peculiarity of Chopin's that, in countless cases, he hesitated not at indulging in covered and even parallel octaves, if by so doing he preserved the contours of his main figures. (See also Example 14 at N. B.)

EXAMPLE 13

EXAMPLE 14

Since the days of Chopin we often hear passages, written
by would-be innovators, that indicate the firm resolve to
forge new harmonies (*i. e.,* discords) at all hazards. They
are, in many cases, produced by superimposing on a given
chord-basis a number of unrelated, unresolvable dissonances.
But this procedure is by no means necessary to create interest,
nor is it indicative of intellectual power.

In Chopin we sometimes imagine we are listening to new
harmonies, but find that they are simply triads and seventh-
chords gracefully decorated. In Examples 13 and 14, from
the *E*-minor Concerto, we have nothing else. At 13b we
have the harmonic outline of 13a, while that of Example 14
is almost as simple. In the latter the changing-notes in the
bass throw a veil over the real chords, but they are always
euphonious, and stand the test of analysis. Again, there are
cases where the illusion is so complete that plausibility begets
credence, and credence conviction, until, on closer inspection,
the fact is revealed that the architect has taken a simple harmonic series and intertwined it with another, containing
regularly recurring changing-notes. (See Example 15, a, b
and c, from the *G*-minor Ballade.)

EXAMPLE 15a

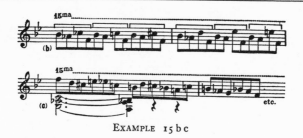

EXAMPLE 15 b c

Sometimes these curious interminglings of dissonances and consonances are not arpeggiated, but struck at once, as in the peculiar passage found in the *Eb*-major Polonaise, Op. 22. Here the result is indeed severely insistent and startling.

EXAMPLE 16

A hitherto unheard-of effect is the tossing back and forth of dissonant harmonies, with their true resolutions, to be sure, but with each chord appearing in an inversion, such as we see in Example 17, from the same Polonaise.

EXAMPLE 17

Example 18a shows the harmonic outline of Example 17.   If
we choose to ignore the influence of the *sevenths,* we might
regard the passage as given in 18b.

EXAMPLE 18

This freer employment of inversions became very characteristic, and Wagner adopted many suggestions of the kind.   A
peculiarly fruitful source of inspiration was the working-out
section of the *B♭*-minor Sonata, where the mood and much
of the melodic outline of the "Götterdämmerung" motive
may be found, as will be shown in another chapter.

Not only did the increased sonority of the improved pianoforte stimulate Chopin's scientific dispersions of triads and

seventh-chords, but the new damper-pedal facilitated the generation of the upper overtones,* and doubtless led to the gradual introduction of more complex harmonies.   He employed the chords of the ninth more freely than did the classical masters, but with altogether new dispositions of the voices, and gave new valuations to the chords of the eleventh and the thirteenth.   These he distributed in a manner quite his own, showing a keen sense of beauty in respect to melodic outline and harmonic euphony.   This may be easily seen and heard by trying over the harmonies indicated in Example 19, selected at random.

EXAMPLE 19

Example 19a is from the coda of the *G*-minor Ballade; 19b is from the second theme of the *A♭* Ballade; 19c is from the coda of the same work; 19d is from the introduction to the Polonaise-Fantaisie, Op. 61; while 19e is from the introduction to the Fantaisie on Polish Airs, Op. 13.† This last is a particularly rare specimen, and might be regarded by some as the first inversion of the chord of the thirteenth,

*Liszt, in a letter to Breitkopf & Härtel, makes the statement that no one indicates the pedal so frequently as Chopin.   I have read that some pianists think that even Chopin's compositions are in many cases mismarked.   Others believe that pedaling is a matter of individual taste.   Huneker says, "The pedals are half the battle in Chopin-playing."   Be all this as it may, the employment of the damper-pedal has, from Chopin's day, become more and more an important factor in piano-playing.   Especially is this the case in the school of Leschetizky, where artistic pedaling has been developed on scientific principles.

†This chord is quoted as given in the Peters edition of Chopin.

founded on the second degree in major.*   But, rich and luxuriant as are these tone-formations, they should be used sparingly, and with circumspection.   The indiscriminate scattering of such treasures throughout a musical work does not imply wealth on the part of a composer; on the contrary, it rather suggests paucity of invention.   Furthermore, they point *too definitely* towards a cadence, and such an elaborate cadence indicates a close, and a close means that one must pull up and begin again, a procedure detrimental to true homogeneous growth.

A still more curious result of experimenting with the higher overtones (for he sets them moving in a fantastic manner) may be found in the return to the theme of the *D♭*-major Étude Op. 25, No. 8.

EXAMPLE 20

This little piece certainly shows itself less dramatic than its sister-études; and Kullak, so enthusiastic about Chopin's

---

*It is difficult, if not, indeed, impossible, to describe certain chords and progressions in such terms as shall be intelligible to all students, owing to the different nomenclatures in vogue.   The effort has been made to make matters as clear as possible, even at the expense of mathematical symmetry. It is to be hoped that those interested in the nature and aim of this work will kindly supply their own technical terms, if by so doing they can make the matter any clearer to themselves and their students.   Personally, I believe in avoiding all needless complexities, and would prefer to reduce these elaborate harmonies to so many suspensions and changing-notes, wherever practicable. At the same time I endorse the scheme of "parenthesis-chords" introduced by Piutti of Leipzig, and advocated by Daniel Gregory Mason of New York.   As the book is out of print, the cnly allusions to the principles advocated by Piutti that I have been able to find, are in the works on harmony by Ludwig Thuille of Munich and Carl W. Grimm of Cincinnati.

great qualities, says, "It is devoid of all depth." But there is always some feature, some novel point, or quaint bit of humor about even the less promising works of this master, which prevents them from becoming commonplace; and this is no exception. Depth it does not have, but there are heights, and the tone-poet has here taken a little flight into the realm of faerie, where the sober laws of madrigal-singing mortals are unknown. The singular series of parallel fifths and octaves one might justify (if it were necessary) as being the result of combining the harmonics of lower tones in such a manner that they produce novel, lace-like designs.

Even the best of composers have occasionally shown marked preference for a given chord. Thus, Mendelssohn was fond of ninth-chords, especially that in minor, while Grieg doted on its major complement. Both composers ran the risk of over-indulgence, but Grieg had a thousand devices in reserve, so that one's attention is diverted before a sense of monotony is experienced. Such favoritism was, at one time, shown by Wagner for the versatile chord of the diminished seventh. Some years since, to gratify my curiosity, I carefully inspected the piano score of *The Flying Dutchman,* and found this chord on nearly every page. Liszt, too, in his piano fantasies, employed it lavishly. Even Beethoven, in the working-out section of the first movement of the *Sinfonia Eroica,* where the Napoleonic conflicts are suggested, gives utterance to whole broadsides of diminished seventh-chords. Bach himself employs this same chord for some six consecutive measures in the Toccata of the *D*-minor Fugue for organ. Mascagni, in the Intermezzo of his *Cavalleria Rusticana,* is fascinated by the chord of the seventh founded on the second degree in major; other composers, of late, are equally hypnotized by its melancholy sister, founded on the second degree of the minor scale. (A young enthusiast once told me he introduced it whenever he found it possible.) Debussy and others who employ the whole-tone scale are enamored of the augmented triad—indeed, here it is a case of Hobson's choice —none other being available.

Whatever critics may have had to say, justly or unjustly, concerning Chopin's works, no one can call him a One-Chord Composer. Listen to the testimony of Rellstab of Berlin, on the appearance of Chopin's Mazurkas, Op. 7. Though hostile, it is eloquent and to the point:

"Chopin is indefatigable, and I might say inexhaustible, in his ear-splitting discords, forced transitions, harsh modulations, ugly distortions of melody and rhythm. Everything it is possible to think of is raked up to produce the effect of odd originality, but especially *strange keys* and the most unnatural positions of chords."

Occasionally, in his earlier works, we find passages in which the chord of the diminished seventh is employed in chromatic progressions. See the Étude Op. 10, No. 3, in the working-out section; the Concerto in *F* minor, for four measures beginning with the thirty-fourth measure before the end; the Romance of the Concerto in *E* minor, cadenza leading to reprise and the Prelude, Op. 45, in the cadenza. But, with the exception of the short passage in the *F*-minor Concerto, the material is so broken up, embellished and woven into airy decorations, that one cannot fail to admire the skill manifested in the effort to avoid monotony. This can be still further concealed (in the cadenza-like portions) by varying the tempi and dynamics.

Patient study of Chopin's works will reveal the infinite care with which he avoided (with the possible exception of the above-quoted instances) anything approaching sameness in harmonic expression. In this respect he is a veritable model of literary style.

Once more let it be emphasized that he is not to be *imitated;* but his conscientious attention to details, and the pains he took to employ, not merely the right harmony in the right place, but the correct dispersion, or even inversion, of that harmony—all this is well worthy of *emulation.*

Bearing in mind the unusually dramatic quality of Chopin's music, it seems quite natural that his friends should have urged him to enter the lists as an orchestral composer. Why he never essayed the creation of opera or symphony, will be touched upon later. (See Section XIII.) To some, his inactivity in this field betokens incapacity. But the ability to write effectively for the pianoforte is, in itself, a gift that ranks with orchestral achievement. Although less cumbersome than the many-voiced organism, this instrument has also its difficulties.*

When, therefore, an artist of the first magnitude devotes his entire energy to expressing himself through the medium of the keyboard, the event commands our attention.

When this artist dominates every detail of this medium, not only differentiating with keen perception the tone-color and shading peculiar to every octave, but also individuating the strength and character of the various fingers, he compels our admiration.

Finally, when he displays a theoretical equipment that enables him to cope with the difficulties peculiar to his thematic material, then, by virtue of this adaptation of the unusual means to the phenomenal end, he awakens our unbounded enthusiasm.

---

*Even Berlioz and Wagner, great as was their orchestral virtuosity, felt ill at ease when writing for the pianoforte.

IV

VIRTUOSITY IDEALIZED

The appearance of Frédéric Chopin marks a new epoch in the history of the Étude; for not only does he offer us a genuine pianoforte-technique of surprising boldness of invention, but even in this form, although designed originally for an external purpose, he also pours forth the entire fullness of his transporting poesy.

Theodor Kullak.

In ancient Rome, gladiatorial combats and struggles with wild beasts in the arena constituted popular amusements long since abandoned in culture-countries, save in Spain and the United States, where we have survivals in the form of contests, involving, respectively, the fate of bulls and bullies. More generally the appetite for danger is sated with exhibitions of skilled acrobats and lion-tamers. So fascinated are the real connoisseurs, that they follow up a performer until he meets with a fatality. So marked has been the progress of the acrobatic art during the past century, that feats which would have thrilled our grandfathers are passed by unnoticed, and the up-to-date artists must devise ever newer and more difficult means of horrifying the spectators. Yielding doubtless to the promptings of curiosity, I accepted, not long since, an invitation to the Circus Busch, in Berlin, where, among other startling features, I saw an alleged belated performer render his equestrian tricks in swallowtail and patent leathers, as gracefully as if clad in his wonted garb. By chance next evening I heard, at a concert in the Beethoven-Saal, a prominent pianist play a well-known composition rearranged for the left hand only. While joining in the applause, I inadvertently recalled Herr Radezky's vaulting in his dress suit. In each case the redoubled enthusiasm was due to the handicap.

Now there are musical critics of high standing who demand that our virtuosos shall make things as difficult for themselves as possible. One recently praised a pianist for playing a Weber sonata at undue speed, "in order to make it seem as difficult as it had appeared eighty years before." Another able writer, an experienced pedagogue, claimed that "in their day the concertos of Beethoven and Chopin had served their purpose, but now, owing to the progress in pianoforte technique, we need more difficult works to meet the demands of the times." This placing so much stress on mere *bravura* is ill advised, for the supersession of the element of quality by that of mere difficulty can never make for the highest in art.

The admiration of intelligent friends is always a source of pleasure and gratification to an artist, and from all that we can learn respecting his tastes, Chopin doubtless enjoyed playing in private, but all exhibitions of pianism for the mere sake of catching the public fancy were distasteful to him. Note Liszt's significant comment in a letter to Wilhelm von Lenz: "Do not forget the etymology of the word 'Virtuoso'; how it comes from the 'Cicerone' of Rome, and let us re-ascend to Chopin, the enchanting aristocrat, the most refined in his magic, quite outside the errors of a school and the silly trifling of a *salon*."

If we glance at the examples given in the last chapter, we shall find that the fascination of the improved pianoforte alone did not suggest them. Such figures and passages could have occurred only to a man endowed with rare pianistic qualifications. The quotations given in Examples 12 to 14 show us that they were written, not by a mere virtuoso, but by a composer with the power to beautify whatever he touched. In perusing a long series of his works, containing complicated piano-figures, one is amazed at the infinite variety displayed in treating practically the same harmonic material. No suggestion of monotony wearies the hearer, nor is he troubled by apprehensions that the fund of decorative devices is in danger of being exhausted. On the contrary, the manner in which the composer elaborates a multitude of novel designs out of the old material is in itself worthy of especial investigation. These features should be played through *slowly,* in order to be thoroughly appreciated. Watch how the most primitive scales, passages and arpeggios, the most familiar progressions of triads and seventh-chords, are recast and given unwonted grace. See how one voice shoots unexpectedly outwards but to return just in the nick of time, thus saving the outline from disintegration. Observe likewise how an additional inner voice is suddenly inserted, often revolving curiously, thus giving a new color to the original figure. All this is sufficient to bewilder the intelligence and dazzle the imagination.

From the very outset, Chopin wrought his chords in a manner unknown to the classical masters. Let us choose as illustrations a few bits from Beethoven's middle period, and a similar number from Chopin's first—the former's Sonata Op. 53, the latter's "Don Giovanni" Variations, Op. 2. In Example No. 21a is a good illustration of Beethoven's arpeggio-work. (See also Op. 27, No. 2, Finale.)

EXAMPLE 21

In Example 22 we see Chopin's treatment of the arpeggio element, at a and b, also (mixed with other matter) at d.

EXAMPLE 22

Melodies or broken chords in simple, undecorated octaves, such as those at 21b, one rarely finds in Chopin; they are always disguised to some extent. (See Example 22b.)* Broken chords, like those for the left hand at 21c, Chopin usually embellishes. (See 22c.) The passage given in Example 23a (*F*-minor Concerto, 1st movement, reprise) may be regarded either as an embellishment of the chords of the dominant and tonic, or as a harmonization of the chromatic scale. At 23b (*E*-minor Concerto, 1st movement, working-

---

*Beethoven, in the first movement of his strikingly advanced sonata in *A,* Op. 2, No. 2, employed octaves similarly broken.

out section) we see a similar treatment of the tonic triad of
B-minor, there being a suspension on the first beat, which gives
it a peculiar charm. At 23c, we have one of those extraordinary Chopinesque specimens of complexity evolved from

EXAMPLE 23

simplicity. This particular example, to use a German idiom,
"seeks its equal." While we seem to hear an incompre-
hensible kaleidoscopic design, the printed page reveals an
every-day scale, but how wondrously freed from all that is
commonplace. Such transformation is possible only to an
inventor of the first rank. Note furthermore that in creating
such forms of beauty Chopin was not compelled to resort to
any of the Oriental scales, or even the chromatic, with which
his name is so often associated. Observe also that one can
never be too careful in analyzing Chopin's compositions, for
even in his episodes and passage-work many a measure, apparently non-essential, proves on inspection to be constructed

with surprising ingenuity. Pianists should bear this in mind;
for, by bringing out the inner voices, which deserve as careful
enunciation as those in a Bach fugue, they will disclose new
beauties otherwise overlooked.

In the more extensive works, written during Chopin's early
period, we notice that the virtuoso element frequently outweighs the value of the themes. This is particularly the case
with those pieces which are accompanied by orchestra. Thus,
the above-quoted Op. 2, the "Don Giovanni" Variations, is
so difficult that it is rarely performed. Indeed, its reputation is due to Schumann's generous enthusiasm, shown in that
far-famed criticism wherein he so happily prophesied a great
future for the composer. The Fantaisie on Polish Melodies,
Op. 13, which evidently owes its origin to Chopin's patriotism,
contains striking beauties, but is seldom played, as pianists
seem to think much valuable virtuoso work is squandered in
decorating themes that are scarce worthy the distinction. In
the Krakowiak, Op. 14, the composer was unhampered in the
choice of motives, hence the result is more satisfactory, all the
elements, melody, harmony, pianistic designs, emanating apparently from one personality, although the flavor of these
themes suggests an ultimate rural origin. In the elaboration
of his passage-work, it is obvious that Chopin sought the
means of beautifying his material less and less in the realm
of counterpoint, and relied more and more upon the charm
afforded by novel harmonic combinations. In the long section,
after the second appearance of the main theme, may be
found an interesting series of harmonic progressions. Beginning as indicated in Example 24, the bass moves downward

EXAMPLE 24

by semitones from $B\natural$ to G. This series of eight measures is followed by two other similar series, in which the bass moves respectively from C to $A\flat$, and then from $D\flat$ to $A\natural$.

It is singular and significant that, when one is in pursuit of a given object, he occasionally attains something unlooked-for, but which is virtually of equal, if not in fact of greater importance than what he originally sought. Here is a noteworthy instance, showing how, in the effort to preserve the interest of his piano-figures, Chopin hit upon a happy device, virtually an extended modulation, which he was able to repeat in a free sequential progression. This feature he had already discovered and employed in his earlier works. It became characteristic of his style, and is the germ of that class of motives to which the term "modulating theme" has been applied.*

In a manner similarly indirect, Wagner derived one of the by-products of his music-dramas. Reference is here made to the quickening of the processes of modulation. This resulted, so the master tells us, from the necessity of permitting the music to follow, as faithfully as possible, the rapidly changing moods of a given dramatic situation. Beginning with modulating themes akin to those of Chopin, Wagner so intensified them that, as he himself said, they would be positively wrong in absolute music. These questionable progressions Wagner justified solely by virtue of their connection with the drama. Many of the master's most vital themes depend upon their harmonic qualities, the expression of a situation being condensed to the combination of but two or three chords. See in the themes of *Tristan und Isolde,* "Desire," "Death," "Tristan wounded," "Tristan doomed," "Day," "Song of death"; in *Die Walküre,* the "Fate" motive, and that of "Eternal sleep"; in *Siegfried,* the theme of "The Wanderer"; and in *Götterdämmerung,* "Hagen's murderous plot," and "Draught of forgetfulness." These motives indicate, in an instant, a

Cf. Section XV, "A World-Force."

thought or mood with a force and accuracy scarcely possible to any other method of art-expression. So subtle, indeed, is the power of these atmospheric portents, that we are tempted to forget their relationship to the music of the classical period.

Some of us do not care for virtuosity, at least we imagine so, but we are very likely to complain if a piece is not played with distinctness and precision. We sometimes forget our obligations to those who have mastered mechanical details, be they vocal or instrumental. To the beautifiers of the former we owe our opera, to the elaborators of the latter, our symphony. From the foregoing illustrations we can learn how Chopin discovered principles invaluable to the growing science of musical theory in the noble endeavor to render the contents of his *bravura* pieces worthy of the difficulties they present, and the audible result equal to the visible display. In Liszt's above-quoted letter to Lenz he alludes very feelingly to this refined quality of Chopin's works, written for the higher order of pianists. The great authority of Weimar writes, "More than this, he sets in motion the heroic string which has nowhere else vibrated with so much grandeur, passion and energy as in his Polonaises, which you brilliantly designate as 'Pindaric Hymns of Victory.' "

Strauss, in his edition of Berlioz's Orchestration, shows how one of the most original and distinctive features in the music-dramas of Wagner was the utilization of the most advanced virtuosity of all the orchestral players.

Bach, Mozart and Beethoven were virtuosos, and if we compare the passages which they wrote for the display of skill with kindred sections from the works of Chopin, we shall find that, while those of the latter often contain less "imitative" work, they are for the most part more richly harmonized, the chords being dispersed in an unusual manner, and the figuration wholly new. With such eloquent testimony in proof of Chopin's musicianship, we are justified in asserting him to be preëminent as an Idealizer of the Virtuoso Element.

V

FIGURATION PLUS INSPIRATION

I look for homogeneity of materials and equipoise of means and ends. Mozart's music and Mozart's orchestra are a perfect match; an equally perfect balance exists between Palestrina's choir and Palestrina's counterpoint; and I find a similar correspondence between Chopin's piano and certain of his études and preludes.

Richard Wagner.

Accustomed to a climate characterized by little or no rainfall, the Egyptian architects doubtless never thought of providing their temples with roofs other than flat. The builders of ancient Greece, on the contrary, living where rain was plentiful, were forced to construct slanting roofs to shed the water, and this mode of structure left a vacant triangular space at either end of their buildings. These gables or pediments afforded the Hellenic sculptors new and peculiar opportunities for the exercise of their imagination, invention and technical acquirements. While the Greeks learned much from the Egyptians, they were thus forced by climatic conditions to develop a new and individual species of structure, although founded on the older forms. One of the most interesting features of architecture is the adaptation of elemental details of construction to the requirements of most divergent conditions. This we find abundantly exemplified in the numerous Gothic cathedrals of Northern Europe, where the conformation of the land, local building material, the political and civic conditions, all combine to affect the form, color and quality of each specimen, while the general type of architecture is preserved.

The same principles may be observed in all normally developed forms of art, and the careful student can usually divine the forces that imparted to a temple, a statue, a painting, a poem or a symphony its individual traits.

We have thus far mentioned the more obvious influences that affected Chopin's music, and shall proceed to a more careful inspection of their operation in his work that gives it that glowingly emotional, yet at the same time chastely intellectual, quality.

But first, in order to appreciate more thoroughly the composer's merits, it is necessary to see what wonders he wrought with the more familiar material—passages and figures which were even then common property. Comparisons made in the friendly spirit of investigation can but conduce to profitable results, and in the present instance they show that Chopin was a master of the art of composition in more senses than one. Play, for example, the studies by Czerny, Cramer and Clementi, for cultivating facility in executing double-thirds, double-sixths and octaves; then place them beside Chopin's Études Op. 10, No. 10 and Op. 25, Nos. 6, 8 and 10. The works of the former are often pleasing, always profitable, but those of Chopin possess the magic quality of making us forget that we are dealing with drudgery.

Again, try his *A*-minor Étude Op. 10, No. 2, where the 3d, 4th and 5th fingers of the right hand execute chromatic figures *legato,* while thumb and forefinger join the left hand in playing the accompanying harmonies *staccato.* Then play through Moscheles's Study Op. 70, No. 3, in *G* major, where the same device is employed, the chromatic work being transferred to the thumb, index and middle fingers. Mark the difference in æsthetic values! This difference is largely owing to the fact that Moscheles places such undue stress on the dominant and tonic in his first period. True, Mozart and Beethoven were often impelled to thus hammer out the obvious, but even Czerny, who at times is a trifle dry, has treated this same technical stuff (in the *Schule des Virtuosen,* I believe) with more poetic feeling than Moscheles, who nevertheless says in his preface, "It is not so much the author's intention to cultivate mathematical perfection, as to address himself to the imagination of the performer."

Chopin's superiority, in the present instance, consists not so much in the mournful beauty of the opening phrases as in the remarkable manner in which, throughout the second part, he winds his plastic figure back and forth from deceptive cadence to deceptive cadence, a device hitherto unattempted, thus extending the boundaries of the original key, to which, however, he returns at the proper moment with a system as original as convincing.

Dickens has been criticized for his melodramatic effusiveness. This was not because of lack of taste or genius. If we stop to realize how long one must wait, even at the present day, for a bit of humor to penetrate the intellectual fibre of a large class of people to whom Dickens appealed, we need not wonder at his being forced at times to "rub it in." In like manner, the musical audiences of a century ago required repeated reminders of the nature of a given theme, as well as renewed confirmation of the key in which it was written. Hence the above comment concerning the hammering upon tonic and dominant by the classical masters.

Chopin appeared at a moment when he could safely rely on a more subtly appreciative audience, one quicker to grasp melody and tonality, thanks to this very training of their ancestors. Not only was the time ripe for a richer development of music, but the receptive faculties of the public were ready for his message. That this message should be made through the medium of the pianoforte was inevitable, for, as I have elsewhere observed, the orchestra in its fullest expressiveness was yet to be evolved.* The chromatic horns and trumpets not having put in an appearance, the *fortissimo* of the orchestra involving the use of the brass was confined mainly to the emphasis of tonic and dominant, the chief stock in trade of the

---

*See Section XIII, "Orchestral Experiments."

so-called "natural" horns and trumpets which give only the series of overtones shown in Example 10.

For this reason we must seek the specifically Chopinesque element in the music of the great Pole, not so much in the elaborate concerted numbers *as such,* as in the more specifically pianistic themes and passages wherever they may occur.

To attempt to categorize them, would be both absurd and difficult; still, were no allusion made to the more important features of the master's creations and no effort put forth to give them some tangible order, a decided gap would result in a treatise which is necessarily fragmentary enough. It may seem to some that in a consideration of the theoretical aspect of Chopin's work too much space is being devoted to what is, apparently, purely pianistic; but inasmuch as the master approaches his art through this door instead of through the choral or orchestral entrances, the procedure may be justified. Among the most individual phases of expression through pianistic means, Chopin employed

A. *Embellished Octaves.*
B. *Criss-cross Designs with Changing Har-*
     ᾽ monies.
C. *Original Chromatic Devices.*
D. *Highly Elaborate Fioriture, Combined with*
     Long Leaps, Irregular Groupings, etc.
E. *Broken Arpeggios with Wide Spanning.*
F. *Double-Notes Mingled with Scale-Fragments.*
G. *Mixture of Chromatic Figures with Leaps,*
     Varying and Symmetrical.

By intermingling these groups, and giving all the subdivisions that would result, this series might be indefinitely extended. It may be regarded as somewhat arbitrary as it stands, but as a tentative outline it will serve our purpose for the present, so a few illustrations under each heading are herewith submitted for inspection.

A. Embellished Octaves.

One of the simpler phases of this type we find in the brilliant coda of the Grande Polonaise in *E♭* major, Op. 22.

EXAMPLE 25

Here the first, fourth and fifth fingers of the left hand perform the lower part of a three-voice harmonic series, producing a sort of tremolo effect.*

An elaboration of this figure occurs in the Polonaise-Fantaisie, Op. 61, beginning with the *B*-minor section. Here the right hand not only must execute the inversion of the figure in Example 25, but thumb and forefinger are likewise involved, rendering the phrase much more difficult of performance *legato*. (See Example 26.)

EXAMPLE 26

The *E*-minor Concerto (first movement) contains a passage in which the left hand is called upon to execute a figure of this type, extended to the compass of two octaves, and is well known to all advanced piano students as being at once charming and elusive. (See closing theme, Example 27.)

---

*Cf. in Section XIV, "Universality," the allusion to this passage and context.

EXAMPLE 27

Kindred passages form a striking feature in the physiognomy of the Krakowiak already quoted in Example 24. Doubtless the most uncomfortable figures of this genus are to be found in Example 28, where the left hand is obliged to play little chromatic groups of four notes each; now with fingers 3, 4 and 5, in the lower register, then with fingers 1, 2 and 3, in the upper. So difficult is this figure when *legato* is demanded, that Scholtz expressed his doubts concerning the adequacy of Chopin's fingering, and suggests another of his own devising,* which is certainly more practicable, although he highly commends Chopin's fingering in general as being notably logical.

EXAMPLE 28

But the discussion of pianoforte technique and the relative merits of various fingerings is not the mission of this treatise. Such matters have been ably set forth by editors and peda-

*See preface to Chopin's works in the Edition Peters.

gogues like Kullak, Klindworth, Huneker, Niecks and others, to say nothing of virtuosos like Liszt and von Bülow. We are at present chiefly concerned with the structure of Chopin's works, and our attention shall now be directed to measures 13 to 16 of the working-out section in the first movement of the *B*-minor Sonata, Op. 58. Here we have (in Example 29) an interesting illustration of how the master takes his curious piano-figures and renders them subservient to the laws of polyphony and weaves them into the "development" of his sonata, after the manner of Bach in his Inventions.

EXAMPLE 29

B.   CRISS-CROSS DESIGNS WITH CHANGING HARMONIES.

Both of the concertos contain specimens of this type. Example 30 is from the so-called "second" in *F* minor, which was in reality the first in chronological order, a fact which the careful student of composition might surmise from the superior grasp of the material shown in the companion-piece in *E* minor. Inspect, by the way, the kindred passage quoted from the latter in Section XV, "World-Force," and notice how much more daring it is than Example 30 in attacking a wide, sweeping modulatory scheme. (*Cf.* Example 92.)

In behalf of the *F*-minor passage, be it remarked that it occurs in the coda, where the object is to render the tonic key

as definite and decided as possible. See, also, the final thirty-two measures of the Krakowiak, where this same kind of figure is employed for a similar purpose. On the other hand, the *E*-minor excerpt appears in the working-out section, where the object is just the reverse—to get away from the main tonality. The comparison was suggested merely to show the technical growth of the composer, with respect to mastering complex harmonic situations. The Prelude Op. 28, No. 5, in *D*, is a beautiful illustration of how the master could evolve from a figure of this sort a complete, artistically rounded composition.

C. ORIGINAL CHROMATIC DEVICES.

The classical masters from Bach on, frequently employed the chromatic scale, sometimes as a portion of a fugue-theme, then in runs, again in the form of embellishments. With his wider modulating outline, Chopin was enabled to make use of the chromatic element in ways quite his own.

Ex. 31 shows three of these figures. At 31a, taken from the Bolero Op. 19, just after the section in *A*♭ major, we have merely a cadenza-like embellishment of a widely dispersed chord of the dominant seventh in *A* major. Observe how indispensable is the pedal to the proper phrasing of this bit. At 31b, however, there is a series of harmonic as well as chromatic, melodic sequences, followed by still another series (31c). The latter moves quite independently of the accompanying harmonies, and the manner in which the composer after all emphasizes the key of the tonic, just at the right

EXAMPLE 31

juncture, is simply bewildering in its mastery of such apparently incongruous elements. Observe, furthermore, that at 31b we have practically 2/4 measure, and that at 31c the figure of four notes is continually repeated in ever ascending sequences. Moreover, the accent falls each time on a different note of the group. This passage from the coda of the Grande Polonaise Op. 22, is repeated twenty-two measures later, and runs into a phase of Example 25. If the student takes the pains to compute the number of pianistic figures in this piece alone, which follow in rapid succession, as if from a never-failing source, he will be able to form something of an estimate of Chopin's inventive powers.

D. Highly Elaborate Fioriture, Combined with Long Leaps, Irregular Groupings, etc.

An excellent specimen of this species is shown in Example 32 (*F*-minor Concerto). Such phenomena are so familiar that they are mentioned chiefly for the sake of completeness.

EXAMPLE 32

We find them usually in the slow movements of the larger works; in the Nocturnes, the Étude Op. 25, No. 7, etc.; but they also appear occasionally in the Polonaises. See, for instance, Op. 22, Op. 26, No. 2, and Op. 53.

E.   BROKEN ARPEGGIOS WITH WIDE SPANNING.

This type of passage, with which diatonic or chromatic figures are occasionally intermingled, is a favorite form of pianistic expression with Chopin.

EXAMPLE 33

EXAMPLE 34

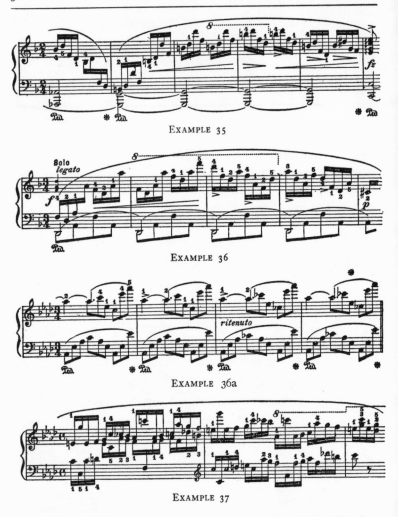

EXAMPLE 35

EXAMPLE 36

EXAMPLE 36a

EXAMPLE 37

In Example 33, from the first movement of the *E*-minor Concerto, will be seen a phase of parallel sixth-chord progressions commented upon elsewhere; it is here rather more elaborately treated, the seventh being thrown in. See Section XIV, "Universality," pp. 162-166, for comments on the principles involved.

Example 34 is from a peculiar passage in the *Allegro de Concert*, Op. 46, the harmonic outline of which is given in 34a. Examples 35 and 36 are from the frequently quoted Krakowiak; while Example 37 is from the Concerto in *F* minor, counterparts of which may be found in the sister-concerto. Example 36a is from the Bolero Op. 19.

F. DOUBLE-NOTES MINGLED WITH SCALE-FRAGMENTS.

Karasowski and Kleczynski rightly remonstrate with that class of foreigners who love to dwell on the delicate constitution, the ultimate illness and the alleged morbidity of Chopin, emphasizing the feminine and ignoring the masculine characteristics of the composer. Kleczynski attributes these complementary traits to the respective nationalities of his parents, hence "Slavonic thoughtfulness and French vivacity. During the period of youth the latter element predominated." This writer believes that Chopin's poetry and sweet melancholy have injured him in the estimation of musicians outside of Po-

EXAMPLE 38

land, and begs us to recall the robust nature that shows forth in the earlier compositions. The masculinity and vigor in the Krakowiak are particularly noteworthy. Here it seems at times as though he had expressed his patriotism in the most joyous manner possible. In glancing through the series of

EXAMPLE 39

extracts from this work (see Examples 38, a, b and c, also Examples 24, 28, 35, 36 and 40), it seems as though a sort of Polish Fourth of July spirit prevails and the composer fires a veritable fusillade of squibs, pinwheels, bombs and rockets.

Students of double counterpoint will do well to examine

the specimen afforded by 38c. First, they should write it out in several inversions, when they will find that the first four measures will come out very satisfactorily in most cases. As Chopin did not intend to use these inversions, he imposed no restrictions upon himself, any more than did Wagner, who in *Tristan und Isolde* gave us several beautiful examples of double and even quadruple counterpoint. This comment is merely to serve as a reminder of what has been already said, concerning the influence of Bach on the young composer.

The *Allegro de Concert* is a number one rarely hears. From the quotations given in Example 39 a, b, c and d, one can obtain but a slight conception of the nature and scope of this opus.

In reading it through, the first two pages impress one as not being up to the master's average; nor does the *bel canto* theme present any specially novel charm. We do not seem to breathe the brisk, sharp breeze of the Krakowiak or the Mazurka, nor the sultry atmosphere of the subtropical Nocturne. No visions of the dancing peasants of Poland, Spain or Italy present themselves, nor do we see the aristocratic society of the Parisian *salon*.

The Beethoven sketch-books in the manuscript collection in the Royal Library at Berlin reveal the remarkable manner in which the master evolved, from rudimentary suggestions and experiments (often of a most unpromisingly commonplace character), those works which fill the hearer with admiration and awe.*

As Nottebohm remarks, he apparently derived his inspiration through labor. Wagner's best themes were born of the

---

*Through the kindness of the Librarian, Dr. Kopfermann, I was permitted to examine the sketches of the projected Tenth Symphony. One finds nothing of especial interest. The theme of the Scherzo is very much like that of the Ninth. But, could Beethoven have been granted two more years, the strength of his youth, and—his *hearing,* he doubtless, from these pencil scratches, would have created a symphonic work surpassing in grandeur his former achievements.

union of poetry and action.   Indeed, he has stated in so many words that, independently of his music-dramas, he was incapable of conceiving a satisfactory theme.   (Witness the Centennial March.)   In an analogous manner Chopin, it would seem, was at times stimulated to creative activity by the fascinating power of unusual pianistic figures, and, as their multifold possibilities revealed themselves, he grew more and more enthusiastic, and the quality of the work became finer and more exalted.   Nowhere do we find a composition that more plausibly suggests his psychological processes.   He apparently intended writing a sonata-movement.   At that day, be it remembered, it seemed necessary to employ, for sonata-themes, figures or motives cast in a sort of four-part harmony mold. Whether this *Allegro de Concert* is the result of an obsession, or a concession, none can say; there is nothing in evidence save the classical physiognomy of his opening theme.

When Chopin by degrees works out of the four-voiced part-writing of the earlier portions, and at length reaches the cadenza, he seems to be at home, and breathes more freely. This is no ordinary cadenza, nor have we to deal with a conventional enharmonic change of the dominant seventh of $B\flat$ to the chord of the augmented fifth and sixth resolving into the six-four chord of A; but we have a $C\sharp$-minor chord (AIII) instead.   An unusual deception.   From this point on, the work grows in beauty and interest.   And it is not without inner qualities of great value; let me call attention to the last appearance of the main theme in A minor.   Singularly mournful and foreboding is this delicate treatment.   If the reader have time and patience to look up that momentous warning of Erda to Wotan, in the last part of *Das Rheingold,* after the words "Weiche! Wotan! weiche!" he will find that Chopin had anticipated the harmonic outline.*

*Since writing the foregoing, I am pleased to find in Ashton Johnson's attractive Handbook to Chopin's Works references to still other features prophetically reminiscent of the Trilogy. See also Section XIV.

This is mentioned here, not to demonstrate Chopin's influence upon Wagner (elsewhere discussed), but to illustrate the fact that he, like all other artists, worked to best advantage when in his own element, and with him this element consisted in those ideal phases of pianism which he himself had evolved. When he was deprived of it, his work suffered.

Particularly happy was the composer in the invention of ingenious chromatic figures, which we see in a new combination under the next heading.

G. Mixture of Chromatic Figures with Leaps, Varying and Symmetrical.

Here again the Krakowiak may be appropriately quoted (see Example 40).

EXAMPLE 40

Example 41 shows a fragment from the Introduction to the Grande Fantaisie on Polish themes, Op. 13. As is the case with all his introductions, this is rich in passages, one following another in quick succession, but so naturally and unaffectedly as to bear witness to their spontaneity. This introduction resembles those of similar works also with regard to the fact that it is equal, if not superior, to the piece it introduces. (*Cf.* Opera 2, 3, 12, 14, 16, etc.)

EXAMPLE 41

The present section shall close with the beautiful cascade of tones from the finale of the Grande Polonaise brillante Op. 22 (see Example 42), and the curious chain of chromatically embellished major thirds in the finale of the *B*-minor Sonata (see Example 43).

EXAMPLE 42

EXAMPLE 43

VI

NOVEL PHASES OF LYRIC FORMS

It cannot be denied that changed conditions produce some, and occasionally a considerable effect, on organisms of all kinds.

Darwin.

In the valley of the Amazon, the visitor following the river, shaded by gigantic trees, looks about him for the far-famed brilliancy of the tropical forest, but is startled by the dreary waste which greets him. Not until he glances aloft does he find the floral display he anticipated. As one writer expresses it: "You are in the empty nave of a cathedral, while the service is being celebrated above in the blazing roof."* The traveler then remembers that the annual inundations have driven the flora as well as the fauna upward. Thus it is that the Brazilian orchids, those proud cousins of our lady-slippers, were forced to learn to live without earth, and subsist upon moisture and air.

The thoughtful lover of nature enjoys doubly the beauty of her inflorescence on learning the relationship of one group of specimens to another, even though he may not have mastered the botanist's phraseology. The artistic layman likewise experiences an intensified pleasure in contemplating the multitude of musical blossoms from strange countries when he realizes how they are modified by the conditions under which they are brought forth. He will notice that in Germany the folk-songs are compact in structure, well harmonized, often showing a symphonic quality in their development from a simple germ. He may possibly observe that in England the popular songs and ballads have a tendency to move in springs of fourths, fifths and the tones that outline the principal triads, thus indicating the sturdy character of the

---

*James Orton, "The Andes and Amazon."

Anglo-Saxons; while it may also strike him that they lack the thematic unity of the German *Lied*.   In France, Italy and Spain the influence of the various Neo-Latinic temperaments is manifest through the grace and vivacity of the melodies. Again, in Slavonic and Scandinavian countries the intervallic peculiarities of the unfamiliar scales and the rhythms of the characteristic folk-dances will impart their respective colorings to the song-forms.

Although the term song-form, associated as it is with naïve verses and simple tunes, brings to mind the more familiar flowers of home, rather than the blossoms of the dense forest, still, in respect to the capacity for conforming to the requirements resulting from a changed condition, the lyric type of structure is more nearly akin to the orchid.   Of this species it has been said that "no plant-form possesses such remarkable powers of adaptation to its immediate necessities."   It takes upon itself the most weird and fantastic phases, yet withal it never denies its family relationship.*

If, in the twenties of the last century, a resident of Vienna, familiar with the works of Beethoven and Schubert, had been told that it was possible to write something new and beautiful in the smaller forms, he would doubtless have listened with incredulity.   And yet on examining the volume of Chopin's Mazurkas we shall find a multitude of details as novel as they are fascinating.

On comparing the Chopinesque treatment of the lyric forms with that of the leading German masters, we perceive a difference so marked as to attract the attention of the most casual observers.   Although the phases that will doubtless first be felt are the peculiar rhythms, melodic progressions and the increased harmonic richness, there is still another feature which distinguishes his work from German models, and that is, the grouping of the measures.

---

*Fegueir, "The Vegetable World" (quoting Dr. Lindley).

In the music of Western Europe melodic symmetry is attained by forming the periods in groups of eight measures,* usually built up from subordinate groups of fours, and twos, but always in such a manner as to give the melody a semblance of continuity. Those who had never heard anything but the music of Italy, Germany or France must have been puzzled or annoyed at some of the Pole's peculiar procedures. That these deviations from Western precedent were inherent in the music of his people, and that his patriotism served as an incentive and also provided a source of new material, are facts often dwelt upon. (*Cf.* Section II.) But that his artistic sympathies were at the same time wide-reaching whenever beauty was to be attained, is evident from his having sought to perfect himself by studying foreign models. Although in his mazurkas the rhythmic conformations are Polish, when he enters the land of dreams—no one could name his nationality. Compare the phrases and periods of the mazurkas in Opus 6 with the opening theme of the Nocturne in *F* (Op. 15, No. 1), or that in *Db* (Op. 27, No. 2). How the melodic lines lengthen in the latter, and how wide is the sweep of the phrase! Here there are no abrupt stopping-places, and one feels impelled to follow the melodic curves to the very end.

On the other hand, we discover now and then, even in the

---

*A word of reminder concerning these smaller forms may not be out of place. These eight-measure periods are, so to speak, used as the basis of our musical reckoning; usually one period closing on the tonic or dominant forms the "first part" (Pt. I) of a song-form, and is followed by another period beginning on the dominant and closing on the tonic, giving us a "second part" (Pt. II). Sometimes a repetition of the first, or even a new part, follows here (Pt. III); but it must close on the tonic. A second song-form, consisting of two or three periods, is added, producing a trio; after which, for the sake of artistic unity, the first song-form (in this case called "main theme") is repeated, usually followed by a coda. For the sake of completeness be it further remarked, that formerly the secondary or contrasting theme was rendered by three voices or instruments, hence the term "trio"; at first specific, it gradually became generic.

classical works of Germany, one-measure members repeated without the variety afforded by interspersing motives of greater length. Witness the Preludes in *C* major and *C* minor in the first volume of Bach's Well-Tempered Clavichord, also the latter portion of the working-out section of the first movement in Beethoven's Sonata Op. 28. Schumann was especially prone to employ a motive of one or two measures with no interruption. See the A B E G G Variations, Op. 1, and the *Kreisleriana,* Op. 16, Nos. 1* and 8, where two-measure members run on indefinitely. In consequence of this procedure he is sometimes criticized for his rhythmic monotony. But how amply does he make amends through the melodic and harmonic beauty of these very pieces! More emphasis should be placed on the fact that there is such a thing as harmonic development which can be made just as interesting as rhythmic development, and even more beautiful.

In following out the analogy between the plant-forms and the musical types with their respective variations, it will be well to treat first the variations in respect to contour (rhythmic groupings, etc.), then those in regard to color (harmonizations, etc.).

To trace the relationship of Polish music to that of other Slavic peoples is no very difficult matter. In one respect it shows a marked kinship to the folk-songs and folk-dances of Russia, namely, in the employment of *reiteration.* Within the realm of the Czar, there dwell not only the specific Russians but a variety of Slavic tribes, with kindred traits of speech and song. In the music of these peoples the habit of repeating a group of notes or a rhythmic figure forms a characteristic feature. The most primitive type of reiteration imaginable is afforded by the chant of the Cossack horsemen, who, as they ride, repeat the following motive *ad infinitum.* (See Example 44.) When intoned by a band of fifty or a

---

*In this instance it is difficult to state definitely whether we are dealing with one-half, whole, or two-measure members.

hundred men, a weird species of nature music seems to fill the air with forebodings of strife and bloodshed.*

EXAMPLE 44

A more advanced species of reiteration may be seen in the ancient Servian motive employed by Tschaikowsky in his patriotic effort to unify into a Pan-Slavic tone-poem a group of themes typical of prominent branches of the great Slavonic race (in his "Slavic March," Op. 30). (See Example 45a.)

EXAMPLE 45

Here there is at once greater melodic and rhythmic variety.†
The other representative themes of the March, although not

---

*The reader may recall those rugged guests of Buffalo Bill, who have appeared in this country from time to time.

†The original is given in Dr. H. H. Parry's illuminating chapter on this topic in his "Evolution of Music." (See Example 45c.)

EXAMPLE 45C

By comparing it with Tschaikowsky's version, it will be seen that the composer was forced to modify its quaint irregularities to suit the exigencies of his work. It will also be noticed that on its repetition an auxiliary figure is added, which seems to suggest the Cossack chant. (See Example 45b.)

exactly reiterative in the sense above implied, are largely built up of one-measure or two-measure motives, each of which comes to a more or less complete close, necessitating a new beginning. This produces the impression of a group of detached utterances, or ejaculations, rather than of carefully thought-out sentences such as we find in the lyric forms of the Germanic peoples. Perfect as illustrations of reiteration are Glinka's "Kamarinskaja" (Russian Wedding Music), wherein a two-measure motive is continually repeated; and the song in Tschaikowsky's *Pique-Dame,* "He Maschanka, kommt zur Linde." In the latter piece the four-measure phrase enjoys a twelvefold repetition. Alternating solo and chorus (with dance), and ever-varying harmonic and contrapuntal treatment, give it the effect of a rustic passacaglia.

Doubtless numerous instances of this reiterative tendency in Chopin's music, illustrating the Slavic kinship of Polish music, will occur to the reader. However, for the sake of completeness, a few examples may be cited from the mazurkas, which afford a rich field for investigation.

The octometric system of constructing melodies, traditional in Western Europe, is for the most part adhered to by Chopin, and in quite a number of instances he builds his periods after the manner of German models; but the more characteristic specimens follow the Slavic system of reiteration in some form or other. Thus a one-measure rhythmic figure repeated may be found in Op. 30, No. 2, measures 17 to 22 and 25 to 30. More striking yet is the trio in $D\flat$ of Op. 50, No. 2, which is altogether built up of a one-measure motive; Part I (8 measures repeated), followed by Part II (8 measures) and Part I again, both of which are repeated. Examples of the repetition of two-measure motives are numerous, as in Op. 6, No. 2, measures 9 to 16; see also Op. 7, No. 3, measures 9 to 24; Op. 24, No. 2, measures 5 to 12; Op. 30, No. 2, measures 1 to 16; Op. 63, No. 1, measures 33 to 40 and 43 to 50.

A perfect illustration of the reiteration of a two-measure melodic figure is afforded by Op. 30, No. 2, measures 33 to 46. (See also Op. 50, No. 3, measures 45 to 60, where the motive is occasionally slightly varied.)

The mazurka does not seem to lend itself to trimetrical grouping, although interesting clusters of six and even twelve measures result from extending or combining smaller groups. (See Op. 33, No. 1, measures 1 to 12; also Op. 6, No. 3, measures 9 to 20; Op. 7, No. 1, measures 1 to 12; and Op. 33, No. 4, measures 1 to 48.)

Four-measure phrases as reiterative motives are to be found in Op. 7, No. 4, measures 1 to 8, and Op. 33, No. 3, measures 1 to 16.

But it is in the grouping of his periods that Chopin's mazurkas so often bewilder us when we seek to analyze them. He could create a complete mazurka from a four-measure group, as is demonstrated in Op. 7, No. 5. The first four measures repeated, slightly changed in the fourth, give the full period. This period repeated in the dominant furnishes the second part, at the close of which is the suggestion "*Dal segno senza fine*," insuring any desired length. The Oriental monarch who demanded a story that should last forever, might have been sated with this curiously distensible specimen, had his taste been musical.

To show the ductility of a single phrase—not in mere repetition but in significant development—we need but turn to the Preludes, Op. 28. What a wonderful mood is awakened by the simple figure in No. 2 (*A* minor). That in No. 9 (*E* major) is grandly rudimentary—only a phrase of four measures played but three times with varying harmonies. No. 20, in *C* minor, consists of but two phrases, the latter being repeated while the reiteration of the monometric motive is heard throughout. No. 7, in *A*, is a single eight-measure period repeated. It may well be doubted if, in a series of pieces of similar length, such great results had been obtained.

But I am to hold to the structural rather than the emotional qualities of these works, difficult as is this self-imposed restriction. Sometimes these shorter pieces assume the garb of the conventional two-part song-form, as in the trio of the $A\flat$ Impromptu Op. 29. Here the second part appears *four* times in succession, but our attention is so occupied with the continuous growth of the decorative figures that monotony is unthought of.

More frequent, of course, is the employment of the 3-part song-form. What can be accomplished within its confines may be seen in the Mazurka Op. 6, No. 4. Such groupings of periods are familiar enough, as is indeed the stringing together of one song-form after another to meet the demands of the ballroom, without reference to regular repetition of given members (see the Waltzes). These forms are essentially terpsichorean rather than æsthetic, and here we might number the *periods* as 3d, 4th or 5th *parts*. For this reason the Waltzes need not further occupy our time or attention. On the other hand, when Chopin, by some bold stroke or peculiar quirk, gives to a single strain the semblance of a full-fledged trio, this is indeed well worth our consideration.

The very first Mazurka of the first group (Op. 6) affords an example of such a rudimentary trio, as does also Op. 17, No. 1; while in Op. 7, No. 1, this embryonic member is repeated in connection with the first part of the main theme.

Again, where a two-part song-form is planned for the trio, one part may be curiously curtailed, as in Op. 7, No. 4.

Much more frequent is the extension of one or both parts of a song-form, as in the above-quoted Mazurka in *B* minor, Op. 33, No. 4, which likewise contains a witty return from the trio to the main theme. (See also Op. 56, No. 1, and Op. 59, No. 3. Note the imitation in the latter.) This method of returning is a customary procedure of Beethoven's, but rarely if ever do we find in the work of this master such a singular coda as is produced by mingling the parts of main theme and trio in the *A*-minor Mazurka, Op. 59, No. 1. Observe how, in this rondo-like number, the second appearance of the main theme occurs in *G* sharp minor.

From the foregoing it will be seen that if we are in search of suggestions concerning musical structure, the group of mazurkas will again prove helpful. At times we are attracted by their exotic qualities, again our attention is called to the principles involved in the development of certain features—artistic transitions, graceful returns, or characteristic codas. Among the latter may be mentioned that of Op. 30, No. 4, with its ambiguous chords V_7 or $\frac{6}{5}\sharp$ chromatically descending. Should one pursue his investigations no further, these specimens will convince him that, throughout the entire range of Chopin's orchidaceous phenomena, there exists a striking diversity of formations, from the graceful to the grotesque.

If the orchids of Chopin's tone-world manifest such unusual variability in respect to the shapes they assume, what shall we say of their coloring? We turn from one surprise to another, and even after half a century, when our modern hothouses offer blossoms of similar beauty, no greater tribute can be paid them than to state that they are Chopinesque. So synonymous is this adjective with harmonic richness, that a citation of specimens were almost superfluous. If the reader will but briefly review the series of examples thus far given, he will feel the full force of this statement.

Nevertheless, the expression of the harmonic element which gives his best works this richness of coloring was not absolutely innate. Like many composers of the post-classical period, Chopin employed modulation quite freely from the very first. Contemporaneous Viennese critics spoke of his writing in the "new chromatic style." From this it is evident that an avoidance of plain diatonic methods was in the air. We need but glance through the Sonata Op. 4 to see that something besides chromatic harmony is necessary to produce a great work. When we compare these tentative phrases, these experimental bits of development and gropings for an individual style, with the great achievements in his Études Op. 10, we realize what gigantic strides he had made. In this group of masterpieces we find the more desirable features of the classical school—diatonic melodies, well-balanced phrase and period-building—together with the richness afforded by chromatic harmonies and modulatory devices heretofore unknown. All these, blended into a homogeneous whole, furnished the basis of a new system of music, a system which we have not yet outgrown, and which no artist employing the tonalities now in existence can afford to ignore.

VII

UNUSUAL COMBINATIONS

> With the new poet everything begins anew, and at the same time
> nothing is interrupted. Each new genius is an abyss. Neverthe-
> less, transmission exists. Transmission from abyss to abyss, such
> is in Art, as in the firmament—the mystery; and men of genius
> communicate their influence, like the stars. What have they in
> common? Nothing. Everything.   *Victor Hugo.*

If Chopin, in his masterly elaboration of the smaller types
of musical composition, apparently defies analysis, what are
we to expect when he combines these forms to produce greater
ones? In piling complexity on complexity, bewilderment in-
creases in geometrical ratio. At least, such is our first impression; and yet, as we listen to the result, the sense of satis-
faction is so complete that we feel that all is well, and we
would not have it otherwise.

Occasionally the traditions of the classical song-form and
trio are preserved,* as in the *G*-minor Nocturne Op. 37, No. 1,
the Étude Op. 25, No. 5, the Fantaisie-Impromptu Op. 66,
and the Polonaise Op. 40, No. 1. In all these instances the
outline can easily be followed despite the occasional extension
of a phrase here, or a period there.

Again, there are cases where the structure is obviously the
same, although certain features are highly ornate and, especially after the "second part" of the main theme or trio, or
both, the progression to the "third part" is rendered interesting by a species of development, a repetition, or maybe a
vacillation and hesitation after the manner of Beethoven.
See the Polonaises Op. 40, No. 2, Op. 26, Nos. 1 and 2, and
the Impromptus Op. 29 and 36.

The æsthetic significance as well as the structural quality
of the first-mentioned Polonaise (in *C* minor) is enhanced by

---

*See Section VI, "Novel Phases of Lyric Forms," page 63.

the manner in which the outer voices of the closing cadence of
the trio are developed until the recurrence of the main theme,
after which the two themes are combined for four measures.
Observe the downward progression of the upper voice and the
upward trend of the bass—*E*♭, *E*♮, *F* and *G*.

EXAMPLE 46

The Polonaise Op. 26, No. 1, in *A* major, might be thus
briefly sketched. Part I of the main theme consists of an
eight-measure period preceded by an introductory group of
four measures, both of which are repeated. Part II consists
of an eight-measure period with a nine-measure introduction;
then follows Part III (Part I minus the introductory phrase).
Parts II and III are then repeated. The Trio is a three-
part song-form with the second part extended. The main
theme is repeated without coda.

The highly dramatic tone-poem in *E*♭ minor, which serves
as a companion-piece to the preceding, faithfully follows the
outlines of the song-form and trio, but the details are so mar-

velously expanded that it breathes forth the spirit of the Sonata rather than that of the *Lied*. The first part (twenty measures of the main theme) might well serve as the principal subject of a sonata-movement. That its iterative character is not inconsistent with the sonata, may be seen by glancing at the opening of Beethoven's Op. 31, No. 3. The equally extended "second part" of this Polonaise (measures 21 to 40) affords material for an excellent secondary theme and sterling passage-work, while the following eight measures might be worked into a "closing theme" of the sonata-outline. The ensuing third part is identical with the first—quite in keeping with the usages of the lyric forms. But, with his consummate mastery of the art of development, Chopin might easily, with the thematic material contained in the first section of this Polonaise, have shown that his technique was adequate to the requirements of sonata-construction.* The expansive properties of this movement may be better realized if we compare the closing cadence (measure 20) with the coda developed therefrom in the last four measures of the work. If the reader be apprehensive lest the imaginary sonata-movement should not be of orthodox length, let him play through the Scherzo of the above-quoted Beethoven sonata. In this delightful *morceau* he will find a sonata-form in miniature.

In spite of the above-cited deviations from convention, the lyric forms remain essentially the same, as we see in the works of Beethoven, who displayed such wonderful ingenuity in the elaboration, extension and contraction of his motives in quest of novel formations. All this Chopin had absorbed, adding to it Slavic rhythms, weird harmonies, and unusual metric groupings. It is worth our while to consider how the last feature affected the shape of some of his best-known works.

---

*See also Section X, "The Amplification of the Sonata Principle."

An important chapter in natural history deals with the abnormal developments of this or that member of certain animals, fitting them for special functions. The extended neck of the giraffe, the lengthened legs of the kangaroo, the elongated little finger of the bat (like that of the prehistoric pterodactyl) with the membrane forming a wing—all these are of practical import. Owing to special æsthetic requirements, due to peculiar rhythmical, modulatory or other conditions, certain musical structures take on unwonted aspects. Already reference has been made to the curious contours given to the smaller forms by combining them with rudimentary trios, episodes, etc. In works with two or more themes, still more startling phenomena are noticeable.

Having developed his unusual faculty of giving variety to a phrase or a period by decorating it with ever richer embellishments, after the manner of Mozart and Beethoven,* we find portions of a theme repeated in another key. In the F♯ Nocturne Op. 15, No. 2, the "second part" of the trio is formed by repeating the first part a minor third higher, with the accompanying harmonies freshly distributed. Observe how this portion is extended and with what a graceful dynamic curve the return to the main theme is effected.

Again, in the less individual Nocturne Op. 32, No. 2, both first and second parts of the trio (respectively in F minor and D♭) are immediately repeated in F♯ minor and D♮ major, and without dropping a stitch he returns to the pattern of the main theme as though nothing unusual had distracted him. All this in twice twelve measures!

If the Chopinesque harmonies afford the grammarians occasion for dispute concerning the methods of analyzing them, the forms of certain works are equally fruitful sources of discussion. The Nocturne Op. 15, No. 1, is a case in which

---

*Kleczynski says, furthermore, that Chopin never played the same phrase twice alike in the repetitions.

two plausible courses might be pursued. We receive the impression of a song-form (first twenty-four measures) and trio (ensuing twenty-four measures—*con fuoco*) after which the main theme is repeated. There is in reality, however, only one three-part song-form with unusually extended periods; but the second part, instead of being similar to or derived from the first, contrasts very dramatically with it.

The Second Impromptu, Op. 36, produces upon the hearer a somewhat similar impression to the nocturne referred to. It seems like a song-form (*F♯*) with trio (*D*-major section) returning to the main theme (*F♮* and *F♯*), followed by a long, highly ornate coda. On the other hand, it might be considered as beginning with an introductory figure (of six measures), after which comes the main theme consisting of phrases extended from four to six measures, the second after-phrase (measures 25 to 30) differing from the first (measures 13 to 18). The portion in *D♮* affords a symmetrical second part repeated with extended after-phrase, while the third part consists of a repetition of the first part (in *F♮* and *F♯* major); then what seems like the coda (the figuration in thirty-second-notes) appears in the light of a trio (and in the tonic, too*), after which follows the codetta of the main theme as "return." Again, in view of the persistent hexametric grouping of the first section, measures 7 to 12 would afford a sort of first part, measures 13 to 18, a second, then part first repeated, then a varied second part, then the codetta; then the section in *D* would be termed a rudimentary trio, after which appear main theme, coda (or second-trio with the thirty-second-notes), and allusion to main theme. However we may view this beautiful work, it is certainly satisfactory, and if the form be doubtful—that is why it is termed "Impromptu."

So accustomed are we to the exalted attitude of Chopin,

---

*The trios of the classical minuets were frequently in the tonic key.

who spared no pains in his devotion to quality, that we are more critical in reviewing his work than we should be in estimating that of another. In this Impromptu the return to the theme in the key of *F* long grated on my nerves, till I learned to appreciate the humor of the transition by means of the doubly diminished triad. (See Example 47a.) Huneker says, "It creaks on its hinges." In fact, were it not for the *A*♭ in the second measure, he would have touched all the keys of the six-tone scale. (*Cf.* Example 47b.)

EXAMPLE 47

In the Nocturne in *G* minor, Op. 15, No. 3, we have the unprecedented instance of a song-form with a trio which never returns to the main theme. Possibly this is a significant phase of the work, composed as it was under the inspiration of a "Hamlet" performance. Chopin, instead of giving the public a hint with regard to its meaning, as was his first impulse, decided to "let them guess."

Within the confines of certain compositions, even where the regular eight-measure groupings of the song-form have been maintained, still other eccentricities are discernible, such as the repetition of the latter portion instead of the beginning of a phrase, to represent the theme. (See the Nocturne in *B,* Op. 32, No. 1, measures 35 and 36.) Here the second part has been curiously elongated until it glides into a recurrence of the sixth and seventh measures of the first part. This remarkable progression (see Example 1 in Section I) is the essence of the period, so Chopin chose to let it represent the first part, and makes no further allusion to the opening phrase. But to search for all the exotic buds, blossoms and fruit of this kind would take us too far afield, so the mention of their existence must suffice.

We listen to a passage written by a master. It may be of such bewildering complexity that it defies offhand analysis; nevertheless we feel that it is the work of genius. Another writer presents something plausibly similar, apparently the same kind of work, but there is a certain raw flavor about it that tells those of true discernment that this man is not equal to the task. Though he may not be what the Germans call a *Pfuscher,* he can at best rank with those termed by Americans the "near-great." On calmly studying both passages, it will be found that the former, no matter how free and bold, will bear close inspection, and stand the test of the best accredited criteria, whereas the latter will not. The master surprises us, not only by his apparent disregard of all rules, but also because of his compliance with the same—in a manner of his own. The moral of this paradox is, that genius comes to fulfill, not to destroy the law.

The mediocrat does neither.

VIII

THE REVITALIZED RONDO

The exaggeration in the panegyrics on everything Greek or Latin, which dates from the classical scholars of the Middle Ages, who knew nothing that could be compared to the classics . . ., continued till, even in our own time, it seemed high treason to compare Goethe with Horace, or Schiller with Sophocles.

Max Müller.

No rule is valid if it impair any characteristic feature of a theme.

Percy Goetschius.

In the dawn of civilization, the difficulty of producing through the medium of the moving arts, poetry and music, impressions as enduring as those created by the static arts, painting and sculpture, must have occasioned much perplexity and annoyance. The memory is obviously more severely taxed in retaining the fleeting tones of voice or lyre than the shape and color of visible phenomena. The latter may be readily fixed through continued contemplation, while the former, no matter how agreeable, are evanescent. Experience showed that the best means of fastening an idea upon the memory was the consociation of words of *similar sound,* producing *rhyme,* and the grouping of words or lines of *similar length,* producing *rhythm.* Hence it is that our oldest proverbs often take the form of rhyming couplets. This humble instance may assist us in realizing how it came about that the art of poetry preceded the art of prose. Even such a master as Chaucer was more at ease in the rhythmic than in the freer mode of expression. As poems grew in length, it was found that a refrain or uniform line at the end of each stanza was an additional aid to the memory. Witness the ancient ballads and our modern topical songs. This led to the employment of a recurrent stanza in which *all* the lines were repeated at regular intervals, to which variety of verse was given the name *rondeau.* An excellent specimen of this form is

Chaucer's "Your yën two wol sle me sodenly," from "The Merciles Beaute: A Triple Roundel."*

> *Your yën two wol sle me sodenly,*
> *I may the beaute of hem not sustene,*
> *So woundeth hit through-out my herte kene.*
>
> And but your word wol helen hastily
> My hertes wounde, whyl that hit is grene,
>   *Your yën two wol sle me sodenly;*
>   *I may the beaute of hem not sustene.*
>
> Upon my trouthe I sey yow feithfully,
> That ye ben of my lyf and deth the quene;
> For with my deth the trouthe shal be sene.
>
>   *Your yën two wol sle me sodenly,*
>   *I may the beaute of hem not sustene,*
>   *So woundeth hit through-out my herte kene.*

By comparing this quaint lyric with the outline of a musical rondo, we see how suggestive this form proved to the early composers.

Main theme = ... 1st Stanza
1st Subordinate theme = ... 2d Stanza (lines 1 and 2)
Main theme (abbreviated) = ... 2d Stanza (lines 3 and 4)
2d Subordinate theme = ... 3d Stanza
Main theme = ... 4th Stanza

So easy is this form to comprehend, as compared with the fugue, that it enjoyed great popularity. No wonder that Bach, in expressing his light esteem for a certain musical instrument, declared "it was fit only for the performance of rondos."

The later classical composers, however, employed it frequently, especially for the last movement of their sonatas. But, as the weight of thought and interest was bestowed upon the first movement (in which the sonata-form claimed attention), the pains and patience of composer and hearers were

---

*"Chaucer, The Minor Poems." Edited by the Rev. Walter Wm. Skeat, Litt.D. Oxford, At the Clarendon Press. 1888.

sometimes spent by the time the finale was reached. Thus the rondo not infrequently received scant courtesy, and the finale rarely ranked with the initial movement. So associated is the rondo with dry and uninteresting material that the very title has fallen into disrepute and is now seldom used. But the form itself, in one or another of its manifold phases, is constantly in evidence. This is largely due to the influence of Chopin.

The advantage enjoyed by the Polish composer in having developed in an entirely different environment from that of his contemporaries, one which had shown its happy influence in his tentative efforts in the lyric forms, soon stood him in good stead when he grappled with the tasks imposed by the more complex and extended phases of composition. The Slavic temperament had not yet found a musical exponent, and Chopin had an absolutely free and fertile field.

Shortly after the death of Tschaikowsky I listened with interest to an able exposition of the difference between the modes of thought and psychological traits of Slav and Teuton by Xaver Scharwenka, at a private gathering. "The Teuton," said he, "builds up everything logically, slowly, surely, in practical matters as well as art and philosophy. Bach, Haydn, Mozart, Beethoven, Schubert, Schumann, Wagner followed each other in measured sequence. The Slavs, on the other hand, progress by leaps and bounds. Russia produced Glinka —then Tschaikowsky."

Some time later I heard Dr. Dvořák express a similar view with regard to the different methods the two races pursue in their creative work.

In the attempts to recombine the lyric forms in such a way as to increase their dynamic force and emotional expressiveness, the rondo shows its kinship with the song-form and trio. In contemplating this relationship one is reminded of those early Italian churches which were supplemented by bell-towers at some distance, both church and tower being architecturally related,* but each complete in itself. This is like the song-form and trio. Again, in the later edifices, where the campanile was incorporated in the main structure, a resemblance to the rondo with two themes is apparent, at least to the extent of showing a more intimate connection between church and tower; while in the Gothic cathedral, so inevitable is the organic unity of spires, nave and transept, that it is difficult to conceive them as separate and detached members.

In order to appreciate the achievements of Chopin in this branch of art, we must see what had previously been accomplished by the musical architects of the classical school.

In his elaborate work on musical composition, Dr. Marx gives a little harmonic outline for young tone-builders to follow in the erection of musical edifices of all forms and dimensions. It is simple enough:

TONIC   DOMINANT   TONIC

apparently too simple. And yet, in looking through the masterpieces of the classical school, the fidelity with which this outline is adhered to is strikingly evident. A simple melody usually begins in the tonic, proceeds to the dominant, thence moves back to the tonic. In longer compositions the first theme is in the tonic, while the tendency of the secondary themes is towards the dominant. After this there must be a recurrence of the main theme in the key of the tonic, in which the piece comes to a conclusion. When the tonic key is minor, the dominant is often represented by the parallel major. This exception to the rule shows that the laws respecting the tonic are more binding than those concerning the dominant. To this, reference will be made later. The importance of tonic and dominant, their relationship and interdependence, was known, not only to the classical composers, but to the Greeks of old and the ancient Chinese.

---

*As in the familiar instance of the Leaning Tower of Pisa.

Nature has steadily asserted the value of these harmonies from the very first.*

We are, furthermore, astonished when we contemplate the vast number of powerful themes that contain little else besides the tones, melodically and rhythmically varied, of the tonic and dominant triads. If we take Beethoven's sketch-books, edited by Nottebohm, and trace backwards the growth of the themes there given, it would seem that he had derived his fire of inspiration from the friction of these fundamental harmonies.

But, although the great masters worked wonders with this simple material, when composers of lighter calibre undertook to employ the same means in a similar manner the charms of tonic and dominant began to fade. To make matters worse, the orchestra of that day was so constituted that these harmonies were always the most prominent features of any composition, no matter how polyphonically thought out.† The trombones, in spite of their capacity for rendering a complete chromatic scale, were excluded from the strictly classical symphony by a custom that obtained as late as the Mendelssohnian régime. The only brass instruments available, therefore, were trumpets and horns of the old type, whose harmonic outfit comprised but two chords, tonic and dominant. Upon these inevitable—though invaluable and indispensable —harmonies, all writers for orchestra were constantly forced to ring the changes, the powerful tones of the brass usually outweighing any ameliorating figurations of strings or wood-wind.‡

*See Section XIII, "Orchestral Experiments," Example 72a, b.
†See Example 72d and e.
‡It may be mere fancy, but I have an impression that Haydn, Mozart and Beethoven did not intend the tonic and dominant to so completely preponderate in their orchestral music, even though due to the penetrating brass. On the contrary, I believe that the f's and ff's marked in the trumpet and horn parts were meant to be merely relative, so as to blend well with strings and wood-wind. The brass, in fact, was added to lend force, color and accent to the general mass, not to serve as a submergent.

The simple grandeur of the classical period was fast becoming cheapened by the imitators who always follow in the wake of any great movement. To save the world of art from stagnation, there arose the masters of the romantic school, without whom the music of the nineteenth century would have been but a mockery and a sham, instead of a fuller development.

Among the important reforms aimed at, by the leaders of this school, were greater elasticity of form, avoidance of long and tedious repetitions, and a release from the thralldom of that *tonic-dominantness* which had grown to be an almost unbearable phase of musical absolutism. The great poets take it for granted that their readers do not require perpetual reminding of the self-evident, and veil in figures that which were otherwise too obvious. So also the romantic composers sought to render music more interesting by lending a delightful indefiniteness to certain passages and dwelling with less persistency upon tonic and dominant.

The classical rondo was so constructed that the main theme was in the key of the tonic, and the secondary themes and episodes in the dominant or other nearly related keys, so that the return to the main theme was always expected in the tonic. This identification of the principal subject with the tonic gave great firmness to the structure. In rondos with two or more themes, the first subordinate theme (together with episode or closing theme, if these were employed) was in the key of the dominant. The main theme (abbreviated, usually) now reappeared in the tonic. Where there was a second subordinate theme, a fresh key was chosen for it—the subdominant, or other closely related tonality. After this the main theme was brought in again, then the first subordinate theme (and other material, if such there were), but now in the *tonic* instead of the dominant, in which they originally appeared. Finally, the main theme further emphasized the principal tonality—usually strengthened by a coda. (See the rondos in Beethoven's Op. 2, Nos. 1, 2 and 3; also in Op. 13.)

Beethoven had already made experiments seeking greater freedom in the choice of keys for the subordinate themes, and, as in the case of the sonata-forms, balanced the wider scope of his modulations by elaborating his codas with interesting thematic work.

Profiting by Beethoven's research, Chopin in his rondos continued to test the values of a more liberal modulatory scheme and a less rigid adherence to the old key-system. In the Rondo à la Mazur Op. 5, so fresh and buoyant, as well as in the Rondo of the *E*-minor Concerto, and also in his Rondo Op. 16 (that seems like a sketch for the same), Chopin tries the experiment of presenting the subordinate theme and the cognate material on their first appearance in the key of the subdominant (instead of dominant), while in the reprise they recur in the key of the dominant (instead of the tonic). I doubt if this would attract the attention of the listener, who would be more interested in the matter than in the method, but whether for the welfare of his work or not, less stress is laid on the tonic at the close, without apparently weakening it.

The Krakowiak, Grand Rondo de Concert Op. 14, is characterized by lengthy episodes, brilliant and richly harmonized, which afford an excellent contrast to the rustic Slavic quality of the main and subordinate themes. The latter appears the first time in the relative minor, the second time in the key of the second degree. It may further be noted that the middle section, beginning in *C♯* minor, is virtually a sort of a development. Already under Beethoven's hands the "working-out" element had appeared in the Rondo, and Chopin used it here as elsewhere with success. At the very close of this piece the main theme appears but briefly and then only in the orchestral *tutti*.

The Rondo Op. 1 is one of the most elaborate as far as

the outline is concerned, though the material is almost classic in its harmonic simplicity, the main theme (like that of Beethoven's Op. 53) consisting merely of tonic and dominant; while Chopin's produces a weaker effect, being built up of one-measure members—a phase of Slavic iteration. As it would be too troublesome to the reader to follow the line of key-relationships, the actual tonalities may here follow:— Main theme, *C minor*. Modulating episode. Subordinate theme I in *E* major (!). Passage in *G♯* minor. Closing theme in *A♭*—Main theme.—Subordinate theme II in *D♭*. Subordinate theme I—first in *D♭,* then in *C* minor; after which the last measures of the closing theme in *C* minor, then the abbreviated main theme with short coda in the tonic, *C* minor. From all this the effort to plan a varied key-scheme is sufficiently marked. The key of *E* for the first subordinate theme is startling enough. After this it was not so easy to find a fitting key for the second subordinate theme, hence the choice of *D♭*. As all the members were of liberal length, there was no room for an entrance of the main theme after the second subordinate theme, hence the abbreviation.

Between the composition of this first effort and that of the Rondo for two pianos (some three years, according to Ashton Johnson)* great progress was made. In the latter work the parts are all well balanced, his longing for rich harmonies is satisfied in a sane and logical manner, while the melodic outlines are graceful and a refined counterpoint is at his command. The outline of the form is clear and simple. Main theme *tonic—C* major; Episode and subordinate theme in *relative minor;* Main theme complete, but the latter portion thrown into *E♭* and extended into a working-out section; then Episode and subordinate theme in the key of the *co-relative, E* minor. New passage-work and coda.

---

*"A Handbook to Chopin's Works," by G. C. Ashton Johnson. London: William Reeves.

But these are not the only rondos written by Chopin, nor are they the most individual. With one who employed the smaller forms with such pronounced success, this form was indispensable. The simplest order of rondo, involving only one theme and passage-work,* lent itself admirably to the building up of certain études. Take, for instance, the one in *C#* minor, Op. 10. The theme (two-part song-form) extends to measure 25, then lengthy passage-work brings in the return 27 measures later. In this final appearance of the theme we are struck by its rapid expansion until it explodes into a coda as thoroughly thematic as if designed by Beethoven. The very next number in the series—the "black-key" étude—is also a remarkable specimen of a one-theme rondo, particularly worth our study, as it is built up under the restrictions imposed by the pentatonic scale. The closing measure of the second part splices on to new passage-work (measure 25), and for the next twenty-four measures the interest never flags. Although the right-hand figure touches nothing but the black keys, the return to the theme in the tonic is startling in its freshness. Praiseworthy, too, is the development of both first and second parts, the latter forming a brilliant coda.

Op. 10, No. 8, in *F*, affords another striking instance. Here the passage (or working out) begins with measure 29. Note the air of uncertainty that prevails just before the re-entrance of the theme. Nos. 6 and 11 of Op. 25 also come under this head.

Rondos with two themes are frequently in evidence, with great freedom in respect to choice of key for the subordinate theme. The rondos in the slow movements are closely akin to the song-form with trio. Particularly noticeable is the affinity between the *two-theme* rondo and the song-form with trio, in the slow movements, where there is little room for ac-

---

*This is according to Marx. Others might regard these specimens as highly elaborated song-forms.

cessory themes and passage-work. In the rondo, the boundary-lines between first and second subjects are less distinctly marked, though even then the impression is often similar to the more detached song-form groups. Observe the various nocturnes, how at times it is puzzling to the student to decide how to classify them. In the Nocturne Op. 37, No. 2, the rondo feeling predominates. Kaleidoscopic in the groupings of its tonal masses, mysterious in its movement, the main theme constantly floats through divers keys, but hovers for a moment on the tonic in measures 27 and 28, preparing the entrance of the trio in *C*. This theme moves more quietly, but is nevertheless ever shifting, drifting on and on, we scarcely know whither, until, without coming to a complete close, it dissolves into the main theme (key of the tonic), which, after sixteen measures, gives way once more to the trio (now in *E*), passing on through a new series of tonalities until the coda, where both themes are utilized and the key of the tonic duly emphasized.

We find the outlines of this form in the Polonaise Op. 22, with broader sweep and much accessory matter, without anything, however, which develops into a second subsidiary theme or even a closing theme, although the bold passage in octaves after the first statement promises something of the kind. But Chopin had a habit of throwing off such an abundance of themes that he frequently employed a new one (possibly not to waste it) rather than use familiar material.

Polonaise Op. 53 is more in the order of the rondo with three themes. After the first statement (introduction and first and second periods repeated), we have the first subordinate subject, or (if you prefer) an eight-measure passage and a period; then the main theme abridged; then the very long second subordinate subject, and the return to the main theme condensed but with a derivative coda.

The Polonaise Op. 44 certainly appears like a rondo with three themes, in spite of the song-form groupings inevitable in a work so dependent upon the dance element. Subsequent to the statement of the main theme a subordinate passage occurs, then the main subject very much shortened; after this, curiously enough, more of the subordinate movement, and finally a very long second subordinate theme (Tempo di Mazurka). Again we have the return of the main theme (including a reference to the introduction) with coda, but no allusion to the first subordinate member.

The Polonaise-Fantaisie, Op. 61, in spite of all liberties somewhat resembles the highest type of rondo, with its three themes, plus a brief but excellent working-out section.

Among the highly idealized Rondos are the Barcarolle Op 60, with introduction, main theme, transition, subordinate theme, closing theme, return of main theme, and coda. Another is the Fourth Ballade in F minor, with main theme, subordinate theme (in Bb), closing theme, return of main theme (highly ornate), subordinate theme (this time in Db), new closing theme and coda.

Each and every one of these masterpieces shows what may be done with the unpromising rondo formulas, provided a man of genius fills in the outlines. It has been shown how the constant tendency to develop from the simple to the complex has increased the expressiveness of music. Before closing this series of analyses, let us review one more number which suggests the infinity of modifications of which the rondo is capable. This is the F-minor Fantaisie Op. 49. Now, we must not be misled by a name.* Here the forms are more freely treated, but they are yet to be traced. After an introduction we have a highly developed rondo-form, with not *three* themes but *many,* which, however, can be grouped in symmetrical order. Let us subdivide the main themes or thematic masses and reduce the bewildering array of melodies and passages to order:

---

*Beethoven's so-called "Moonlight" Sonata is termed *quasi una Fantasia,* but its forms are perfect, though unusually grouped.

Introduction, 42 measures.

Main Theme A, 25 measures; B, 9 m., *Tonic.*

1st Subordinate Theme C, 8 m., *Relative Major;* D, 8 m., *Modulation;* E, 16 m., *Dominant of the Relative Major.*

Episode or Passage F, 18 m., *Dominant of Relative Major.* Closing Theme G, same key; 16 measures.

Development-Section A, 12 m., *Modulation.*

Development-Section B, 9 m., *Minor Dominant;* C, 8 m., *Sixth degree of Subdominant.*

Development-Section D, 8 m., *Modulation;* A, 19 m., *Modulation.*

2d Subordinate Theme Part I, 8 m.; Part II, 8 m.; Part III, 8 m., ($B\natural = C\flat$).

Reprise, beginning with A 12 m. (new phase modulating). Then follow B, C, D, E, F, and G—note for note, measure for measure in keys a fourth above, *Subdominant and Relative Major—* after which the Coda, A, 10 m. (as in Development for 6 m.).

2d Subordinate Theme 2 m., plus Cadenza.

Main Theme 11 m., *Relative Major.*

It will be seen from the above that strong sonata traits are manifest, as is sometimes the case in the Beethoven rondos. Without wishing to institute comparisons, which would show that Beethoven's work was more compact, and also that Chopin's possessed higher harmonic value and greater melodic charm than the typical Beethoven Rondo, we are justified in suggesting that even in respect to form Chopin influenced his successors, by demonstrating the possibility of enriching and beautifying the song-forms and the rondo. This is obvious in the works of Bizet, who shows not only the influence of Chopin in his forms and harmonies, but also that of Bach and Mozart in his counterpoint and Berlioz and Wagner in his orchestration.

One reason why *Carmen* possesses such unusual enduring qualities is because Bizet had the gift of writing clear-cut melodies which he combined in the most effective manner. In this work are numerous song-forms with trios, also certain rondos. One of the latter constitutes the "Seguidilla" woven about the dialogue between Carmen and Don José. Here we have Main Theme, variously interrupted, broken or ex-

tended by the Subordinate Themes in the guise of recitatives
and lyric phrases.

One invaluable feature of the Revitalized Rondo is that delightful wavering about indefinite tonalities before the reappearance of the principal theme in the main key. Although
this device has already been mentioned, the student will do
well to observe how Bizet applied this principle in the return
from the second to the third part of the main theme in the
"Seguidilla" above quoted. How elusive and expressive of
Carmen's coquettish remarks! (See measures 68 to 82, out-

EXAMPLE 48

lined in Example 48.) By the way, who would think, on
hearing the introduction to this number, which seems to establish the key of *F♯*, that *D* major is the real tonality? Here
we have to do with a highly decorated cadence.

The Quintette in Act II is a gorgeous specimen of rondo,
robust and rollicking, relieved by subordinate themes of
lighter calibre which do not impede the progress of the movement. We even have development fragments thrown in here
and there. The work is well worth studying from the standpoint of musical form, to say nothing of the orchestration.

Max Müller, in his Autobiography, relates how when a
boy he experienced a feeling that his teachers were inclined
to "somewhat overpraise" those works that claimed a classic

origin. At the same time, they allowed the achievements of modern writers to pass without proportionate recognition. Many of us have noted a similar tendency in the musical world. Whatever bears the stamp of classicality passes for its face value; that which shows the imprint of a later period must stand severer tests.

In the *G♭*-major Étude in Op. 25, Chopin employs a figure strikingly similar in contour to the opening theme of the *Vivace* in Beethoven's Sonata Op. 79, which is worthy of a moment's serious consideration.

Now it so happens that von Bülow considers this charming Étude to possess little musical worth, and says, "The amiable commonplaceness of its melodic content reminds one of the style of the late Charles Mayer." This dictum serves to show the advantage of being a classic writer, for otherwise a commonplace theme bearing the name of Mayer would be thought just as ordinary if signed by Beethoven.

EXAMPLE 48*bis*

In the light of this evidence it certainly is permissible to claim for the works considered in this section a value equal to that of anything of the kind produced in the classical era, and if they may lack any attributes which one finds in the old-school music, they possess, on the other hand, qualities which were unknown to the public of the rococo period.

IX.

FRESH PATHS THROUGH OLD FORESTS

The subject-matter confronts every one; the contents is discovered by him who has the requisite gifts; while the form is a secret to the multitude. *Goethe.*

SIR CHARLES RAMBLETON. But mind you, sir, though great our debt to William the Conqueror for planting New Forest, methinks that he who reveals the beauties of a fresh thoroughfare thro' the same, is hardly less worthy of our gratitude. *Old Play.*

In the endeavor to free his mind from care and worry, the weary tourist seeks the relief afforded by unfamiliar scenes. More than this, he takes pains to diversify his rambles from one objective point to another by following unfrequented byways, such as abound in the Thuringian forests and Tyrolese mountains.

In preparing his itinerary through the realm of tones, Chopin, while beginning in the main key and returning to it at the close, after passing through nearly related tonalities, contrived to maintain interest in the airy voyages by means of excursions into out-of-the-way paths, and in so doing often made short cuts through side-lanes little known or visited. He thus in his invisible scenes imparted to familiar phenomena a sense of never-ceasing novelty, which in a measure accounts for the strange fascination they exert.*

If we would do full justice to Chopin's achievements in the

---

*Beethoven had already begun to vary the classical formula which prescribes the appearance of the subordinate themes in the dominant (for major sonatas) and in the relative major (for minor sonatas). See his sonatas, Op. 13, Op. 31, No. 1, Opera 53, 57, 90, 106 and 111. More than this, he showed how the interest increased in direct ratio to the suspense awakened concerning the ultimate direction to be taken by a given figure in returning to the main theme in the main key. In this respect Chopin was the legitimate successor of Beethoven, applying these principles to more elaborate material, frequently within smaller compass. That Bizet was in line with both these masters may be seen by glancing at Example 48 in the preceding section.

field of harmony we must not rest satisfied with mere admiration of an individual chord-formation, or an isolated modulation, no matter how attractive. We should go deeper, and examine those passages that reveal deliberate, premeditated planning of elaborate transition from one tonality to another. After studying these carefully we shall learn that Chopin felt not only profound respect for tonic and dominant, but possessed a keen appreciation of the relative importance of the affiliated keys and accorded to each its essential value.

While these various attributes are obvious in the majority of his works, large and small, they are particularly noticeable in the Études and Preludes, owing to their remarkable compactness, rendering it relatively easy for us to follow the curves taken by these modulatory by-paths. Furthermore, on inspecting these works, we see that the means employed in the transition from one section to another are ever-varying. The student would do well to analyze the entire series, bearing this in mind. He will find that Chopin remains for the most part true to the traditions of the song-form. This is usually clearly outlined, the cadences of the first part being such as to mark the key, but at the same time the composer frequently closes on degrees of the scale seldom thus employed. When more conventional cadences are made use of, variety is obtained by beginning the second part in a relatively different key. To emphasize this fact a series of first-part endings and second-part beginnings of a number of Études and Preludes is herewith subjoined. (See Table, Example 49.)

It would only bewilder the reader were an attempt made, in a brief survey like the present, to give the character of every cadence, whether complete, incomplete, deceptive, compound, feminine, or what not. Furthermore, considering the conflicting views of standard authorities, it would be inadvisable to state too definitely the length of certain periods or the precise instant that the real close of a given cadence has taken place. In the elaboration of his piano-technical figures

Chopin often sought to give them the greatest semblance of continuity, and this was best effected by means of delayed resolutions, simple and compound suspensions, and deceptive cadences.

ÉTUDES FROM OP. 10.

	CLOSE OF PART I.	BEGINNING OF PART II.
No. 1. (*C*)	1st time in key of V. 2nd time in key of I.	In key of VI (relative minor).
No. 3. (*E*)	1st time in key of V. 2nd time in key of I.	In V of V (dominant of the dominant).
No. 5. (*Gb*)	1st time in V of VI. 2nd time in......V.	In V of V.
No. 7. (*C*)	In ....III.	V of II (dominant of key of II degree).
No. 8. (*F*)	In ....I.	IV closing in V.
No. 10. (*Ab*)	1st time in......V. 2nd time in......I.	VI of tonic minor (*g♯*), closing in IV; then repeated in VI of IV minor (*c♯*).
No. 11. (*Eb*)	Twice in..........I, modulating to	VI of tonic minor.

ÉTUDES FROM OP. 25.

No. 1. (*Ab*)	1st time in key of V. 2nd time in key of VI.	V of VI (dominant of the relative minor).
No. 3. (*F*)	Twice in............I.	V through various keys to the V of *B♮* (=*Cb*).
No. 8. (*Db*)	In V, modùlating to..	VI (relative minor).
No. 9. (*Gb*)	In.................I.	V.

PRELUDES FROM OP. 28.

No. 17. (*Ab*)	1st time in........V. 2nd time in........I.	V of II with fundamental lowered-phase of Neapolitan 6th (*A♮*=*Bbb*).
No. 19. (*Eb*)	1st time in V (chord of 13th). 2nd time in........V.	V of relative major of tonic minor.

EXAMPLE 49

From this table it will be seen that even to those cadences which are essential to the establishment of the main key, much variety is given; and that a comparison of those that are apparently similar in this respect, will reveal important differences. Thus the first part in Nos. 1, 3 and 10 of Op. 10 is repeated, each closing the first time in the dominant, the second in the tonic; but No. 1 modulates to the key of the dominant outright (though its entrance is accompanied by a suspension), while No. 3 barely touches the dominant in passing, and No. 10 merely grazes it, *via* the minor ninth. The second endings are also varied. No. 1 has a complete, No. 3 a plagal, and No. 10 a feminine, cadence. (This last term implies a close on the weaker, or less accented, portion of the measure.)

But it is in the second parts of these pieces that the composer has full scope for the exercise of his phantasy and ingenuity; many of them, indeed, assuming the character of working-out sections, as we find more fully illustrated elsewhere.* In the shorter études, where this is neither practical nor necessary, Chopin lends new contours to the song-form: 1st, by repeating the second part in a new key; 2d, by extending it through development; or 3d, by adding new and kindred phrases.

In the $A\flat$ Étude, Op. 10, from No. 10, the first method is employed. Here the second part in E major (VI of the tonic minor) is continued till it closes in $D\flat$, the IV of the main key. This new key is dwelt upon until we have been impressed with its import. Then, changing to minor, it introduces the repetition of the second part in A (VI of the subdominant minor).

In the F-major Étude, Op. 25, No. 3, not only is the second part repeated, but also the first, in quite new keys, giving a still richer and more bewildering aspect to our simple song-form. First, we observe the great pains the composer has taken to emphasize the main key by closing twice in the tonic. This is in order to balance the unusual amount of modulation that ensues. Beginning in the dominant, through a series of sequential transitions, the second part is brought to a minor plagal cadence on $F\sharp$. The dominant of $B\natural = C\flat$ — the II degree of $B\flat$ — IV of F major with fundamental lowered. (See Example 50.)

Cf. Section X, "Amplification of the Sonata Principle."

EXAMPLE 50

The first part is now repeated in the new key (B♮), after which the second part appears once more, beginning in the dominant (F♯), and through the same series of modulations transposed an augmented fourth below, the return to the first part in the tonic is effected with as much grace and simplicity as originality and boldness.

Études Nos. 2, 5, 9 and 11 from Op. 10, and Nos. 1, 4 and 9 from Op. 25, show how the second parts may be extended through a consistent development of the themes and figures in question.

Especially interesting are No. 9 (analyzed in section on "Unique Structural Problems") and No. 11 of the Op. 10 group, in respect to the development of harmonic themes. The student will do well to compare the latter with the A♭ Nocturne by Field. Here we may have to do with a mere coincidence, or possibly a case of unconscious cerebration. Be this as it may, the first thirteen notes of the theme suggest the opening measures of Field's work, if we combine the upper voices of the latter, but Chopin's version at once takes on new color and form and his *conscious* cerebration is such as to distance all rivals. In the second part, especially where he makes use of a complex harmonic motive, we have that which is quite new. Observe the brilliant two-measure sequences ascending by whole steps, then the one-measure sequences descending so gracefully, followed by an organ-point on the dominant, with the imitation between the two upper voices and a rich progression of harmonies leading back to the repetition of the first part. Also observe the coda, in which new phases of the motive are evolved with a logic as uncompromising as if Beethoven himself had designed it.

The $A\flat$ Étude, which opens Op. 25, has a fascinating second part which, beginning in the dominant of the relative minor, moves about until we find ourselves in the key of $A\natural = B\flat\flat$, where we seem likely to remain until, by means of some spell, the transformation is effected and we are brought, after all, to a close in $A\flat$.

To show how, through the addition of new material to the second part, it may be so extended as to correspond to the æsthetic demands of the work, we need but refer to Études Nos. 6, 7 and 12 of Op. 10, also No. 6 from Op. 25. These additions may be in the nature of new derivatives from the original figures. This is the case with the above quoted Études from Op. 10, also in the Prelude Op. 28, No. 17, in $A\flat$. The modulatory outline of the last is worthy of especial attention.

A diagram of the études in minor would show at least as great variety of key-combination as is presented by those in major. But in order to indicate the true values of these tonal undulations, it would be necessary to give so many supplementary details that the result would be confusing to the reader. For this reason a more thorough analysis of fewer specimens will be substituted.

The F-minor Étude No. 2 (Op. 25) is structurally noteworthy owing to the fact that, although it is a two-voice movement throughout, it produces the effect of harmonic completeness.* Another feature is the development of the second part from the final measures of the first, which con-

---

*See also the first étude of the group written for Moscheles and Fétis; also Prelude No. 19, in $E\flat$.

sists of a double period closing in $A\flat$ (16th measure extended
to the 19th). This portion is repeated and closes again in $A\flat$
at measure 35. Here occurs a witty splice, the final measure
(or measures—35 and 36) being employed as the germ of a
four-measure phrase, the sequence of which (a tone higher)
is followed by an organ-point on the dominant. The long
slur that practically encloses the entire work shows that from
the phrasing alone one can obtain no definite idea of the
structural divisions of a composition.

The Étude in *C* minor, Op. 10, with its well-known message of grief and despair consequent upon the Polish national disaster of 1831, has been frequently discussed and in-
terpreted. It sounds at first, indeed, like an uncontrollable
ebullition of righteous wrath, but this, too, will bear the
closest inspection despite von Bülow's comment on its "chromatic meanderings." After an introduction of 10 measures
the first part (8 + 2 measures), closing in the tonic, is repeated, closing in the dominant of the relative major ($B\flat$,
V of $E\flat$). The second part begins with the subdominant
minor of the relative major ($G\sharp = A\flat$ minor — IV of $E\flat$).
A sequence one tone lower brings us to $C\sharp$ ($= D\flat$ minor),
then by upward sequences through untouched tonalities, skill-
fully avoiding too remote keys, back to *C* major (V of *F*
minor). (See Example 51.)

EXAMPLE 51

Then a passionate outcry in *F* minor, a new phrase, taking us
to the opening of the third part, repeated, and followed by a
bold harmonic design (apparently in $G\flat$ major, but in reality
the Neapolitan 6th in the second instead of the first inver-

sion), followed by a sequence one tone lower. (See Example 52.) After this, a suggestion of mournful contemplation (passing from $E\flat$ to C minor) is supplemented by a coda in which the stormy left-hand figures die away;—a final explosion brings us to the tragic end. All is developed consistently from the thematic material with which the work begins.

EXAMPLE 52

As an illustration of the dramatic possibilities of the humblest material, let us consider Chopin's mastery of the commonplace as exemplified in the $G\sharp$-minor Étude, Op. 25, No. 6. Nothing could be more homespun than the progression of two voices in parallel thirds, as treated by hundreds of composers, yet when woven by the hand of genius, and intertwined with other voices, this humble fabric takes on the quality of silk and satin. See measures 11, 12, 14, 15, 18, 23, 27, 28, 43 to 47, 51 and 52. Witness the remarkable sequence of the beautiful double parabola in measures 43 and 44.

The simplest way of proving Chopin's phenomenal capacity for finding new methods of proceeding from one objective point to another is to compare any two of these Études that chance to be in the same key, and observe their marked diversity. Thus, in the middle section of the F-major study in Op. 10, the composer establishes an organ-point on A, while in the kindred study in Op. 25 the goal to be gained is B major. The climax of Op. 10, No. 1 (C major), is the dazzling series of sequences throughout the diatonic scale; while in No. 6 of the same group (same key) the interest

centres upon the means of getting back to the tonic after an
organ-point on the dominant has been reached and abandoned.

But in all probability the most striking dissimilarity ex-
hibited with regard to methods of modulation may be found
in the Études in *A* minor, Op. 10, No. 2, and Op. 25, No. 4.
In the former the second part begins with the V_9 of VI
(Dominant 9th of *F* major) (*F, D♭, G* minor, *E♭*), from
here to *A* minor, back through *F* and *E♭* to an organ-point
on *E*, thence to the return of the first part in the tonic. (See
Example 53.) In the Étude from the later opus, the composer closes his first part in the seldom used key of the minor
dominant. The second part opens with a modulating sequence, the first section (two measures) closing in *F*, the
second in *D♭*, six-four position (meas. 22). The bass, after
sustaining the *A♭* for several measures, ascends chromatically

EXAMPLE 53

EXAMPLE 54

to *C* (V of *F*) in measure 27. After wavering about till
measure 30, this section closes in the unusual key of *C* minor,

changing in the vacillating extension to *C* major, which leads more naturally to the key of the tonic, whither the first part returns in measure 39. On its repetition this singularly hesitating figure works itself into an appropriate coda and close.

During the past seven or eight decades these unique compositions have inspired and charmed thousands upon thousands of listeners, who have felt the pulsations of what seemed like impassioned, spontaneous improvisations. But a reasonable amount of study will show that the architectural qualities are in every respect worthy of the themes themselves—indeed, are inextricably involved in the same. In Example 53 we have no less than four harmonic designs, and in Example 54, two. Almost any of these outlines is of sufficient value to enrich compositions of serious import and of greater length. For the sake of conciseness these sketches are much compressed, Example 53 representing seventeen measures, Example 54, twenty-one. On comparing these skeletons with the completed structures, it will be seen how Chopin varied rhythmically his harmonic designs. Here he extends them, there he breaks them into shorter members, and again he repeats a measure or a fragment of a phrase. (Note the alternate use of *D♭* and *D♮* at N. B., Example 54.) But it is all done with reference to the ultimate arrival at the objective point.

Charming as are the colors and moods of some of the musical impressionists, there is a tendency to let their lines run together into a blur. This blur is cultivated to such an extent that some believe true musical progress to be identified with an increase of dissonant qualities. However, such is not necessarily the case. A recent German critic writes, "What are we to do? Even the most frightful discords fail to attract." On the other hand, when a man has the ability to find fresh paths through old forests, it sometimes consists in giving a semblance of remoteness to keys closely related.

From the well-worn rut between tonic and dominant within

the eight-measure period, we find that Bizet has made a most unexpected deviation in the very beginning of *Carmen*. Observe the ingenious, roundabout manner of approaching the key of the dominant in the fourth measure; then note the sense of surprise occasioned by the sudden spring into the appar-

EXAMPLE 55a

ently foreign tonality of the subdominant. Had Bizet written this phrase forty or a hundred years previously, it would have taken on a form somewhat as suggested at 55b.

EXAMPLE 55b

This simpler harmonic outline would not only have been more in keeping with the order of the classical themes, but the primitive nature of the old trumpets would have sternly dictated the same.*

There is a manifest endeavor on the part of many of our modern theorists to bring their text-books into line with the achievements of the past few decades. Not only are modern writers quoted in connection with the classics, but newer, perhaps unsuspected kinships of keys are divined and indicated. To the latter feature much attention is paid by Piutti, Thuille

---

*See Section XIII, "Orchestral Experiments."

and C. W. Grimm. The last goes so far as to show that all chords are related, and gives appropriate names for their relationships. He refers to the essay read by Fétis in 1832, putting forth the hypothesis that "some day proof would be given that all chords were to be found in every key." It is interesting to learn that Liszt was present and was deeply impressed with the idea, which stimulated him to further experiments; but I venture to suggest that M. Fétis was very possibly led to make his statement after listening to Chopin's Études, for we remember that the latter contributed three very characteristic ones to the Method of Fétis and Moscheles. These contain curious instances of plausible relationships between quite remote tonalities.

X.

AMPLIFICATION OF THE SONATA PRINCIPLE

Not of the Letter, but of the Spirit; for the Letter killeth, but the
Spirit giveth life. 2 *Corinthians iii:* 6.

Every book is written with a constant secret reference to the few
intelligent persons whom the writer believes to exist in the million.
R. W. Emerson.

In glancing through the musical literature of the Post-
Beethoven epoch, one finds a goodly percentage of the compositions cast in the mould of the sonata. But to what purpose the form, where the material so meagrely warranted the
effort? One is reminded of certain mountainous districts of
California, honeycombed with abandoned mines. The ex-
pert is frequently compelled to admire the engineering skill
displayed, many can appreciate the industry, while all deplore
the barrenness of the results. After contemplating the achievements of Bach and Händel, Beethoven was not constrained
to devote his energies to the production of more fugues and
oratorios. He wisely decided to exploit a sonata-mine instead, which he left pretty well exhausted; and there is small
occasion for wonder that Chopin sought his fortune in other
localities.

When one's first knowledge of Chopin has been derived
from hearing and studying the Polonaises, Mazurkas, Preludes, Nocturnes, etc., the thought of his composing a sonata
comes as a surprise, it being so apparently incongruous to
associate his wealth of phantasy with pieces so often characterized by harmonic, yes, even thematic aridity. Not until
one has heard the transcending beauties and the dramatic
outbursts of the Chopin sonatas evoked by pianists of the first
rank, is it at all probable that such ideas of incongruity give
place to enthusiasm for Chopin's evident mastery of this
form. Then one finds that he was able to make it suit his

needs, discarding that which was non-essential and suggesting new possibilities for the future—possibilities of which comparatively few have availed themselves. But, when such avowedly friendly writers as Liszt, Karasowski, Ehlert, Finck, Niecks and Huneker note Chopin's preference for freer forms, we can easily understand why writers less kindly disposed assert his incapacity to create works bearing the sonata imprint. His Op. 4 is one of his least interesting efforts, and was obviously nothing but a study in sonata-form, which the composer never intended for publication. Indeed, shortly before his death he requested his friends to destroy it, together with other works truly beautiful (the Rondo for two pianos, the Fantaisie-Impromptu Op. 66, the *E*-minor Waltz, etc.). However, this first sonata is an interesting experiment, and the strictures one reads concerning it are as undeserved as the absurd comments on the composer's fugue which somebody played in Berlin a few years ago. Such studies in form are indispensable to a beginner, and subsequent works give evidence that Chopin profited by the experience. The lack of rhythmic variety in the first movement disappoints us in none of his later writings, nor does he again persist in such perpetual modulation to no particular purpose; furthermore, he never indulges in so much conventional thematic work—quite overdone here, in fact. At the same time, we find many pleasing passages and one very valuable invention which he elsewhere elaborated to good purpose.

He had already hit upon this device of letting a series of chords of the sixth follow each other in rapid succession along the half-steps of the chromatic scale, in his "Don Juan Varia-

EXAMPLE 56

tions," Op. 2. It is interesting to see how it came about. First they appear as a series of inner voices, while the outer tones are practically sustained. (See Finale, measures 32 to 35.) Then, further on (measures 49 and 50), the chords move freely, but within the boundaries of the key. The Polonaise for Pianoforte and 'Cello, Op. 3, which contains a kindred passage, was written the year following, while three years later he employed the device to excellent purpose in his *E*-minor Concerto. (See Example 56b.) *

EXAMPLE 56b

This brief digression seems permissible, inasmuch as it strengthens our impression that almost everything Chopin wrote contained some feature of interest even where we least expect it, and shows that he had much valuable new matter which, had he confined himself to the writing of sonatas, might have resulted in many beautiful works. This alone would have created a new style. But, far better as it was. Chopin's standpoint with respect to this order of composition was that of the devout believer in the tenets of a religion, who at the same time has outgrown some of its formalities. He was not one who sought to create a schism,† but rather one who wished to render the ritual more pliable and adapt it to the needs of a varied constituency. Occasionally worshipping as a churchman, but more frequently as a nonconformist, he was able in both cases to attest his sincerity and the genuineness of his convictions. Chopin, like the prophet of old, had breathed upon and rehabilitated the dry bones of

*Cf. Section XIV, "Universality," for later and more remarkable evolutions from this germ.

†He did not care to be considered a Romanticist.

the Étude. Was it not possible that he might also galvanize
the cadaver of the sonata, this once vigorous form which had
been reduced to a state of inanition by masters and mediocrats
of the classical school? The composer's efforts are certainly
worthy of our serious attention, and the result will show that
our opinions respecting his ability in this direction should be
subjected to a thorough revision. The young Pole who
brought with him such a wealth of new material—beautiful
melodies, harmonic and rhythmic features which fastened the
attention of the hearers at once—had found his natural expression in those forms that best fitted his individual contributions to art. The Étude had attracted him, not because of
its barren past—enabling any one to become prominent who
could cause it to assume the guise of poesy—but because he
saw that the new instrument was capable of a thousand fascinating figures hitherto undreamt of. More than this, by com-
mitting himself to no predetermined plot or plan, whch one
must follow in writing rondo or sonata, the Étude, by virtue
of its amorphous character, offered him free scope for his
fancy. In the first movement of the Bb-minor Sonata, we feel
the spirit of the Étude at the beginning, bold and brilliant as
it is, for the same rhythmic figure continues during some thirty
measures. But monotonous it assuredly is not. Listen to the
harmonic development! And the moment we picture to ourselves the hero riding on to battle, we feel it could be no
other way. Now comes the lovely lyric theme—quite out of
place in an Étude—followed by a closing theme of great vigor
and ever tenser harmonic action, bringing us to the double-bar.
And then? We have a repetition, a custom that long obtained
in the orthodox sonata-form. In this instance we enjoy the
continuation of a mood, which is virtually necessary for so
broad an outline. Still, had Chopin not promised the public
a genuine sonata, he would in his own inimitable manner have
given us a far more continuous and vivid picture. But what
has he done? In spite of formal fetters, he plunges boldly

into the working-out section, combining the fateful *Grave* theme with that of the rider, to which he adds a new lyric phase (measure 17, and again at measure 25). Just here, in the most structurally difficult section, his inspiration soars to its greatest heights. In the fury of the conflict we hear harmonic designs never before conceived; harmonies which, as before mentioned, are akin to those Wagner employs in *Siegfried* and *Götterdämmerung*. To drop from this altitude, and repeat the entire first section, would be unfortunate indeed for the artistic movement of the piece. Wagner, in his essay on Liszt's symphonic poems, expressed regret that Beethoven, in complying with convention, repeated the first section in the great Leonore overture. This repetition, he asserted, impedes the flow of the otherwise highly dramatic music. Chopin wisely omits the thoroughly exploited main subject, and introduces the lyric theme at this point in the usual key (tonic major). The number then proceeds to a satisfactory close. The intense mood generated is projected into the following Scherzo, which is wrought out in its every detail in a manner impossible to one not thoroughly master of the sonata-form. So absolutely did Chopin absorb the *spirit* of the sonata in its deepest significance, so completely did he acquaint himself with every device known to the craft, that all his greater works became *sonatafied*. He was not obliged to give each time the complete outline, main, lyric, closing theme, working-out section, reprise and coda, to show his familiarity with this form. But whatever he did contained the element of the *working-out* or free fantasia, with numberless details such as subtle progression of inner voices, sometimes with delayed resolutions of dissonances, harmonic designs and modulating themes; features which greatly increased the difficulty of treatment, as compared with the simple melodic curves of the classical school.

Chopin has been criticized by Jadassohn, Niecks and others for the disposition of his secondary theme in the first movement of the *E*-minor Concerto. According to custom, it should stand in the relative major (*G*), in the statement, whereas Chopin brings it in the tonic major here, and in *G* in the reprise—exactly the reverse of conventional usage. Inasmuch as the composer had already manifested such unusual skill and taste, in the simpler forms, as to fascinate many and frighten others, it seems as though his essay in the more elaborate methods of expression should be treated with respect and consideration, especially as there was no falling off in the quality or originality of the themes and other individual details. We are justified in assuming that Chopin was capable of studying the standard models, and of adjusting the means to the ends in the concertos, as well as in the smaller forms.

We have seen how careful he was in maintaining a balance of power between the tonic key and the modulating portions. In the *F*-minor Concerto (which, as before mentioned, was written first) he showed his knowledge of conventional methods, for the secondary theme appears in the relative major (*A♭*). Undoubtedly, the adoption of the tonic key for the first announcement of the lyric theme of the *E*-minor Concerto was the result of due deliberation or strong intuition. As most of his themes modulate very freely, many of them, indeed, depending upon modulation for their character, this unusual procedure indicates a desire to lend stability to the key-scheme by emphasizing the tonic.* This method he also applied in his chamber works.

If we compare any kindred classical work with this *E*-minor Concerto, we can realize Chopin's anxiety to accentuate the main key. Witness the startling modulating figures in the working-out section, such, for instance, as is shown in Example 92 in Section XV. This passage is preceded by eight

---

*In the scherzos of his first four symphonies, Beethoven brings the trio in the tonic; merely taking pains to touch, in the digressions, different keys from those employed in the main theme.

measures in *A* minor. After the sixteenth measure of this quotation, the preliminary eight measures together with the nine-measure group of Example 92 are repeated in a series of keys a fifth higher (or a fourth lower), bringing us to new figurations. No less than three attractive patterns, beginning in *C♯* minor, carry us gracefully and convincingly to the dominant organ-point. We must not overlook the thematic allusion. In the coda appears an extraordinary phenomenon, an epoch-making feature. This is the modulating theme shown in Example 93 (Section XV).

When we realize that Chopin was a mere boy at the time, and from his letters seemed even to doubt the merits of this work, we can form some conception not only of his great mentality but also of his unusual modesty, for the harmonic outlines and pianistic figures shown in Examples 92 and 93 have scarcely been surpassed in boldness, beauty, or brilliancy. Note the logic with which the modulatory scheme is maintained, and how variety and unity are obtained by breaking section *a* of Example 93 into members *b* and *c*.

It would be interesting and profitable to analyze all the greater works, not only those avowedly cast in the sonata-mould, but more especially those in which no pretense is made of following the classical outlines, for the latter are nevertheless enriched and ennobled by sonata elements. The Scherzos, Ballades, the Études, especially Op. 10, Nos. 4, 6, 8, 10 and 12; Op. 25, Nos. 1, 6 and 11, and even certain Nocturnes, such as Op. 32, No. 1, Op. 37, No. 2, and Op. 62, No. 2, are most suggestive. In all of them we find either clear-cut working-out sections, codas highly developed, or the second part of the song-form taking on the character of the free fantasia, if not actually supplemented by it. Possibly, instead of examining more complex material, it will be better to turn our attention to the more familiar examples afforded by the Second Scherzo and the Third Ballade. In recalling to mind the ever-beautiful, though much abused *B♭*-minor

Scherzo, it may be stated in brief that the themes in the tonic
and relative major are repeated, followed by the pastoral and
strong rhythmic motives in *A* major, *C♯* minor and *E* major,
which are also repeated, closing with an eight-measure arpeggiated figure indicated at Example No. 57f.

EXAMPLE 57

Although this piece, as is the case with the other scherzos
and ballades, presents a freely woven rondo-design, we may
say that at this point the "statement" ends. We are made
familiar with all the material and at once enter upon a
"working-out" section (as in a sonata), introduced by a development of motive *f*. First, we have another eight-meas-

ure period (chord of the seventh on the second degree of
A minor), followed by four-measure phrases, also developed
from motive *f,* with a figure in the bass derived from motive
e 1, continually modulating and bringing us to a free fantasia
on motive *e,* for twenty-four measures. Here we meet, after
a deceptive cadence in *F♭* major—enharmonically, the
E-major chord of the 6/4 (fourth and sixth),—introducing
motives *c* and *d,* the latter developed into passages which lead
into a new treatment of motive *e.* This in turn is elaborated
into a brilliant and effective working-back to the main theme
by means of a diatonically descending passage with peculiar
insistence on tonic and dominant. Such a procedure is unusual, for the tonic, as a rule, is saved up for the reëntrance
of the expected theme. Still, we cannot wish it otherwise,
and precedent exists in Beethoven, who, in his *B♭*-major Symphony, leads to the reprise with an organ-point on the tonic
alone. Brahms has followed this in his Sextette in the same
key. Chopin now brings the main themes in *B♭* minor and
D♭ as in the beginning; at the close jumping into the coda
by means of a deceptive cadence—motive *c* 1. Beginning in
A major, modulating back to *D♭* major (*più mosso*), motives
a and *b* (the latter intensified into motive *g,* and later *g* and
h), this sonata-like coda closes with a brilliant development
of motive *c* 1, to which has been added another factor, *c* 2,
derived from the progression *d,* and now playing a most important part in ascending to the climax, as may be seen by
playing the last twenty-four measures. After tracing this
relationship, the student may find it interesting to play over
the entire coda (beginning in *A* major) with especial reference to motives *c* 1, *c* 2, *a* 1, *b,* *g* and *h.* This last passage
gave great offense to some of Chopin's admirers at the time
it was written, owing to its dissonant qualities, but the justification lies in the fact that they result from a natural growth,
and are not thrust in arbitrarily for effect. In closing be it
remarked that the student should not fail to notice the de-

velopment in the twenty-four measures before the section in
A major, also when it appears in the reprise.

As before intimated, the popular Third Ballade contains
structural elements of interest. Although the themes are
conceived in a mood poetic and fanciful, we find traces of
the sonata-form of more than ordinary value. Beginning
after the close of the first section in *A*♭, the second theme
(Example 58b) now appears in *D*♭ major, introducing the
working-out section. This is followed by motive *c* of Example 58, now in *C*♯ minor, with a florid counterpoint in
16th-notes, down to the figurated organ-point on *B*. Up to
this point the succession of themes is, relatively, much the
same as in the statement, in spite of embellishments, but now
comes something quite new. We have ten measures of
organ-point on *B* breaking into a chromatic run in the bass.
The first six of this group are devoted to the second theme
(see Example 58b) ; the following four, to the first theme

Example 58

(Example 58a). Then follows a sequence ingeniously dove-
tailed into the first upon a *C* organ-point. The two themes
next alternate in groups of two measures each above an
organ-point on *D* (four measures), then a sequence of four
measures on *E*♭. This last organ-point, being the dominant,
is extended by four measures with a development of motives
a^1 and a^2 (Example 58), which brings in the main theme
quite after the manner of a sonata reprise. Chopin, however, feeling that the material did not call for a complete
repetition of everything, first develops his main subject for

a few measures and then brings in a final allusion to the tributary theme with the sweeping arpeggios, and closes by means of a rich and comprehensive cadence. Before leaving this beautiful specimen the student should read through the opening eight measures, then the seventeen preceding the entry of the second theme (58b); by comparing these passages with motives 1, 2, 3, 4 and 5, an idea of Chopin's thematic development may be obtained.

The Second Ballade, in *F*, opens in folk-song mood, interrupted by a *Presto con fuoco* in *A* minor, closing with a deceptive cadence on an organ-point ornamented with scale-like figures, which are woven about the low *E♭* for fourteen measures.* These figures gracefully resolve into a reappearance of the rural theme in the tonic. Here we have the beginning of a working-out, or elaboration of this quiet melody into dramatic episodes. The *Presto* appears again. Note how the rural theme (this time in the bass) is combined with the former just before the Coda (*Agitato*), Tempo I°.

In the *G*-minor Ballade a unique introduction† dissolves into the main theme, followed by a sort of middle section or tributary theme, also in *G* minor; a secondary subject running into a closing theme much on the order of the sonata appears, both being in *E♭* major. With the succeeding reappearances of the main theme in *A* minor (organ-point on *E*), a virtual working-out section begins, closing with an organ-point on *B♭*, apparently to bring us to the reprise. But no! Quite new material in the key of *E♭* major greets us, and, after more modulating, we meet the secondary theme also in *E♭*, as it appeared before with its closing theme. Obviously, this form is only slightly related to the sonata, but it has the *vital element,* the working-out section, as predicted, and also a coda that brings back the main theme in the tonic (organ-point on *D*), developed as Chopin has frequently done, following Beethoven in this respect. That the new material in

---

*See Example 67, p. 137. †*Cf.* Section XIV, Ex. 81.

$E\flat$ was found in the working-out, or, if you choose, replaces the main theme, is merely one of those liberties which the composer allowed himself in these romantic forms. The codas of the first three ballades and those of all the scherzos should be studied with an eye to their organic development.

The Fourth Scherzo in E major presents an amazing amount of work of this nature, and is worthy to rank alongside of Beethoven's sonatas with respect to homogeneous evolution of given material. While the motives are light and fanciful, not in the character of sonata-subjects, the workmanship is thematic throughout. Observe the skillful return to the main subject by means of a trill-like figure ingeniously interwoven with the theme itself from time to time, and reappearing in the coda, where it develops new and unexpected beauties.

From the foregoing illustrations it is evident, that no matter how beautiful one's melodies and harmonies may be, their value is greatly enhanced by a wise application of those principles which render the sonata, in its *broadest* interpretation, one of the most significant creations of man. After making these studies, we come to the conclusion that we have been inclined to overlook the fact that the sonata element pervades the greatest of Chopin's works, even when he had apparently "cut himself adrift from all bondage, and floated at his own wild will."

Few of us, while attending a performance of *Tristan und Isolde* or *Siegfried,* stop to consider how monotonous the most beautiful leading themes would become were they constantly repeated without elaboration or amendment. How is it that they preserve their power and increase in interest? Because the poet-composer was able to infuse into these motives the element of growth by virtue of his mastery of the Sonata Principle.

XI

UNIQUE STRUCTURAL PROBLEMS

Some men are becoming aware of the fact that archæology is not architecture. *James Fergusson* ("History of Architecture," 1883).

Chopin's creation was spontaneous, miraculous. He found it without seeking, without forethought. It came suddenly—complete and sublime, as it sang itself in his head during a walk, and he hurried to hear it himself by giving it to the piano. Then began the most terrible labor I have ever witnessed. *George Sand.*

This little theme 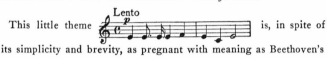 is, in spite of

its simplicity and brevity, as pregnant with meaning as Beethoven's

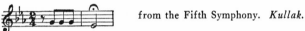 from the Fifth Symphony. *Kullak.*

There is ever a semblance of the supernatural about genius, which appeals to all save the cynical and the blasé. We surrender ourselves to its mysterious charm, and enjoy the illusion that men blessed with extraordinary gifts are not subject to those laws that govern the actions of ordinary mortals. Even late in life, Liszt, whose enthusiasm was unabated, refers to Chopin in a private letter as "an incomparable genius, whose work as an artist remained transparent, marvelous, ethereal. . . . He is akin to the angel and the fairy." Of the same psychic manifestation Ehlert says, "He appeared suddenly, like a mirage, whose evanescence and fantastic form delight us, and about whose origin we puzzle our brains."

We are sometimes inclined to resent the attempt to account for these rare phenomena, dreading lest the effort belittle their grandeur, or render too tangible their subtle qualities. Nevertheless, investigation is here, as elsewhere, profitable, for it enables us to demonstrate that these enchanting apparitions are not at variance with the system of our universe. On the contrary, they are proved to be merely the result of the deflections of known forces from their wonted channels, or unusual manifestations of unbroken laws.

Some years ago, while walking down one of those hilly streets which characterize San Francisco, I was startled by the appearance on the steeply inclined pavement of the sky, trees, and moving objects, reflected in the trembling air heated by the summer sun. A step, forward or backward, and the illusion was lost, but when the line of vision was parallel with the smooth pavement of the downward incline, the mirror afforded by the palpitant ether created a perfect mirage. The mystery of the *Fata Morgana* was solved; but that did not destroy its beauty.

Dannreuther, Scholtz and Finck refer, quite as a matter of fact, to Chopin's influence on Schumann, Liszt, Wagner, Grieg, Bizet and many living writers. This implies not the mere borrowing of a stray chord, cadenza or passage, but the employment of new principles which he discovered. We are, therefore, as fully justified in the endeavor to ascertain the nature of this "new vision and new version of beauty,"* as we are in studying Beethoven's sonatas and symphonies in the light shed by the master's own sketch-books edited by Nottebohm.

At the outset we must note certain survivals of the classical methods and touch upon their discontinuance. Ehlert apologizes for the few examples of canon and imitation afforded by Chopin's works. He quotes with great pleasure the example, in the C♯-minor Mazurka Op. 63, of canon in the octave, declaring that it "could not have been more perfect had he grown gray in the learned arts."† This is as though, on finding an acrostic or a *rondeau* by Kipling, our doubts concerning his genius should be dispelled. It is singular that Ehlert did not hit upon the imitation in the *F*-minor Ballade

---

*Dannreuther.

†See also the Mazurka Op. 50, No. 3, first period.

and that in the Barcarolle.   The coda of the latter would lose much of its charm, if the imitation in the middle voices were lacking.   (See measures 13 and 14, also measures 9 and 10 before the end.)   Possibly these features were experiments of Chopin's in his later period, to see whether it were not possible for him to enrich and vitalize the canonic element as he had already the contrapuntal.   Compare the counterpoint to the secondary theme in the Rondo for two pianos (written in early life, but marked Op. 73) with that which we find in the nocturnes or in the Études Op. 10, Nos. 4 and 12, or in Op. 25, No. 7, and observe his progress.   The contrapuntal lines in the Rondo are of severe, Romanesque simplicity; those in the later works are so elaborate that they suggest the Flamboyant Gothic.

Hermann Scholtz, whose excellent work in the Peters edition shows his devotion to the master, wrote, in an otherwise highly appreciative letter to Karasowski:

"One thing which we frequently miss in Chopin's compositions (especially those written in large form) is the thematic work, in which (for example, the principal features of Beethoven's creations) the spirit of the old masters is chiefly to be sought.   One pardons a little defect of this kind in an artist as rich in phantasy as Chopin, in consideration of his undeniable excellences, so much the more since he opens a new world of thought to us, and so completely soars aloft in the creations of his imagination; most of his shorter works therefore make rather the impression of an improvisation."

Now, as Chopin was preëminently thematic and his works are full of the most elaborate development of that character of motive which was so peculiar to him, it seems strange that his workmanship should have escaped this able editor. Doubtless he missed the alternation of themes and the transplanting of a melodic figure from one register into another, which one finds in Beethoven so frequently.   (See the working-out sections of Beethoven's Sonatas Op. 2, No. 2; Op. 26,

No. 2; Op. 28; Op. 31, No. 3, etc.) And yet, although the specifically Chopinesque themes neither demand nor are especially favorable to such treatment, we do nevertheless find splendid illustrations of it in his works. Thus at the very beginning of the Third Ballade, the bass in the fifth measure repeats the theme announced by the soprano in the first. An excellent development of this motive in the bass, accompanied with harmonies ever growing to suit this development, we find further on, in measures 41 to 44. This is answered by the upper voices taking up the strain (measures 45 to 47). Observe also the extension of the motive F-$E\flat$, in measure 46. In the following measures we hear the soprano melody of measures 7 and 8, given in the bass. Again, nothing could be more "thematic," and effectively so, than the passage beginning in $C\sharp$ minor, where the closing portion of the theme in F minor appears in the bass, while the soprano takes the inverted organ-point $(G\sharp)$.*

The Second Ballade likewise contains some beautiful polyphonic development of the opening (F-major) theme, on its first reappearance after the presto. Here the motive is taken up by one voice after another, in a manner which Beethoven could scarce improve upon, and appears dramatically announced in the bass (measure 17 of the second presto) accompanied by figures such as only Chopin has given us. Other instances might be cited, such as the working-out sections of the Second and Third Sonatas (first movements), the trio of the scherzo in the latter, and especially the first two movements of the Sonata Op. 4. Indeed, this contains so much conventional thematic work, that we realize it was written as a study, and that Chopin had not yet perfected his own style with its peculiar methods of evolution. Note also the splendid antiphonal work in the $C\sharp$-minor Étude in Op. 10, and the coda of Op. 10, No. 11. (See measures 25 to 32; 44 to 51.)

*Cf. the analysis of this work in Section X.

That Chopin perceived, at the very outset of his career, how effective certain chord-progressions may become when accelerated, is evinced by measures from several of his earliest works. The Polonaise Op. 71, No. 1, written (it is said) when he was but seventeen years of age, shows how he had already begun to experiment with this sort of material.

EXAMPLE 59

Compare this example with the progressions of diminished seventh-chords in the working-out section of the opening movement of Beethoven's Heroic Symphony. Since this acceleration has been introduced, it would seem as though Liszt and Wagner had pretty well exhausted the possibilities of the diminished sevenths ascending or descending chromatically. In this connection be it said once more, with emphasis, that the rapidity of chromatic work should not be overdone. Time is required for the sound-waves generated by each chord to impress themselves upon the ear, and when this required interval is not allowed, the result is a jumble of tone—or rather noise. This deplorable result is frequently achieved by pianists who race through the works of Chopin, or by conductors who tear through Liszt and Wagner.

An editor who had a keener insight than Scholtz into the real merits of Chopin's workmanship was Kullak, whose bold attitude is shown in the quotation that heads this chapter. A careful inspection of every detail of the great *A*-minor Étude would be as profitable to the student of theory, as are its technical details to the pianist. The pregnant motto that "like a scarlet thread is drawn through the brilliantly flashing waves of tone and which, as it were, prevents them from scattering to all quarters of the heavens," Kullak has given above, while the figure, or rather figures, that accompany it, may be seen in Example 60.

EXAMPLE 60

On comparing Examples 60 and 61 we shall find wherein the accompanying figure consists of two voices instead of one, and, on playing through the entire Étude with sufficient cir-

EXAMPLE 61

cumspecticn, it is evident that the composer confronted a fourfold problem. This consisted, *first,* in a logical development of the march-like motto; *second,* the development of the outline afforded by playing the first, third, fifth, and other alternate notes of the figuration (see Examples 61, a and b); *third,* a like treatment of the outline resulting from playing the other series of alternate notes—the second, fourth, sixth, etc. (see Examples 61, c and d); *fourth,* the preservation of all these members without permitting them to clash or interfere with each other. The master furthermore renounced the relief afforded by a trio, or contrasting theme, in a piece ninety-six measures in length, at the same time avoiding all sense of melodic, rhythmic, harmonic, or formal monotony. So completely did this powerful intellect conquer these apparently insuperable difficulties, that the result seems like a brilliant improvisation and the average hearer bestows no thought whatever on the processes involved in its construction. This is doubtless the effect the master desired, but unfortunately here, as in many kindred instances, Chopin's remarkable structural virtuosity so blinds the every-day workman, that the vital elements of homogeneous growth and formal proportion are quite overlooked. Hence, it is not impossible that, even with the strains of this very masterpiece ringing in his ears, the listener may find himself giving credence to the familiar statement that "Chopin had style, but no form." Such is only too frequently the hypnotizing power of presswork over the evidence, that we feel the force of the Frenchman's proverb, "Art is noble but criticism is holy."

When examining the details shown in Example 61, the eye is attracted by the symmetry of all the members. Motive *a* consists of a chromatic scale, running downwards through four octaves; motive *c* is the inner voice in the form of a broken arpeggio. The figure *b* follows in the fifth measure and is essentially simple beyond belief, but when its tones are scattered through three octaves combined with the bold figuration, *d*, one scarce realizes that it forms a feature of this wild spray of tones. (See Example 60b.) The same motive (61b) is made use of at *e*, combined with the harmonically significant lines at *f* and *g*. At *h*, it is wrought out in so ingenious a manner, that it may be regarded as creating three groups of four tones each, four of three tones, or six of two each. The structural outline is that of the three-part song-form, the second part being supplemented by new developments of these various motives creating the impression of a sonata-like "free fantasia" or working-out section. This is necessary in this instance, as in some of the other Études (see Op. 25, No. 6; Op. 10, Nos. 3, 4, 6 and 8), to give that variety usually afforded by the trio or second subject (as in Op. 25, No. 5), but which would here needlessly break the flow of the "waves of tone."

The rhythmical development of the various sections is also most consistent. After the four introductory measures, we have an eight-measure period (2+2+1+1+2) closing in the dominant. This is repeated, the last member being extended so that we have a ten-measure group closing in *C* major. These eighteen measures are next transposed to the minor dominant, the second part of the song-form, closing the first time in *B*, the second time in *C*, the close attained by different means from those employed the first time. With the opening of the working-out section, the left hand takes the figuration, and the right the main motive, for four measures. Then begins a series of startling modulations, which produce that sense of unrest so very typical of the ideal *free fantasia*, in order that we may enjoy the pleasure of observing how the composer brings his theme back to the home key after all its wanderings. The opening measures show the march-motive in the right hand; the left hand in measures five and six takes it in a modified form and modulates to *A♭* major; measures seven and eight (a sequence) bring it to *E* major. Notice how the harmonic progressions now coincide with the metrical development, for here follow four one-measure members, respectively A V_7, C minor, Db V_7, E *minor*. Then comes a two-measure group in which the harmonic rhythmic members grow smaller, F V_7 for a half-measure, then six quarters devoted respectively to the chords of F I, E minor V_7 and I, D minor V_7 and I, and A minor.* One measure, chord of A minor, $II°_7$, another of E V_7 and we reach the organ-point on E (dominant of A minor) for twelve measures, but the last eight are so gracefully disguised that we hardly feel it. This brings us to the third part (a repetition of the first part), which in this case feels like the reprise in a short sonata-movement. Measures 15 and 16 of the reprise present a weird figuration of the chord of the augmented fifth and sixth; measures 17 and 18, a still more remarkable scattering of the tones of the augmented sixth, fourth and third chord; measures 19 and 20 elaborate the sixth and fourth cadence, ushering in the last outbursts of the main motives. Notice how Chopin now brings in his motives separately; first the figuration (Ex. 61, *a* and *c*) for four measures, then four more devoted to the "march-like motive." It will be seen that the introduction of the latter rhythm in connection with the figuration (as Kullak suggests) would be out of place and an anti-climax.

On reviewing our analysis of this typically Chopinesque work, we find that it embodies mental qualities rarely combined. It recalls what Dr. Lübke says concerning Moorish ornamentation: "These arabesques testify to the restless imagination and the profound, speculative (*grübelnde*) minds of the builders."

Beethoven's remarkable faculty for creating much out of little, evolving a symphonic movement from a few notes, was counted unto him as righteousness. If that were a virtue in Beethoven, why not in Chopin?

_____

Cf. outline given in Example 90, p. 170.

The *F*-minor Étude (Op 10, No. 9) is a noteworthy evolution from a very small germ—two notes and a rest (see Example 62, *a*1). How inevitably the second half of the opening measure (*a*2) follows the first (*a*1). As unavoidably does the second measure succeed the first, and with the added impetus continues until the phrase closes on *C,* in the fourth measure. This phrase is repeated and the melodic curve widened, closing with the motive *e,* which the old school theorists would surely regard as a diminution of *b.* This eight-measure period, forming the first part of the song-form, is repeated, closing in the tonic. The organ-point having been retained for sixteen measures, it is refreshing when the second part takes on the nature of a modulating motive; the first phrase closes in *A*♮ major (chord of the sixth), the second in *D*♮ major (chord of the sixth and fourth) ; but with motive *d,* the composer moves right on through *D*♮ minor

EXAMPLE 62

into a series of modulations that continually increase in rapidity. Note how this is in keeping with the development of the shorter and shorter motives, *viz., a b* and *e.* After this outburst we must quiet down, catch our breath an instant (organ-point on *C* with motive *f* varied). Then comes the third part with new modulations and developments of motives *a* and *e,* but never leaving the organ-point on the tonic; while the coda is formed from the motive *f,* showing that Chopin had not only learned the art of development from Bach and Beethoven, but also how to economize, for he utilized to the utmost his thematic material, wasting nothing.

After this Étude has been thoroughly analyzed and its essence absorbed, the student will do well to follow the building processes employed in the Études Op. 10, Nos. 7 and 11 ;

Op. 25, Nos. 4, 8, 9, 10 and 12; also Preludes Op. 28, Nos. 1, 8, 12 and 14.   He cannot fail to admire the genius that evolved such wonderful structures from simple one-measure motives.

This combination of compactness and great expansive powers entitles them to rank with the themes of Bach's inventions, preludes and fugues; nor is their development less exemplary.

From the foregoing it may be seen that a new element has entered music, something the classical masters had not encountered, namely, quickly moving harmonic masses.   To manipulate successfully this feature requires the utmost pains and conscientious criticism, in order to avoid smeary melodic outlines and smudgy tone-combinations.   In order to obtain the full value of these passages, they should not be performed with undue haste.   As Kullak says, "A too rapid performance

EXAMPLE 63

deprives the listeners of the possibility of following attentively the architectural construction.   In the case of Chopin, such a deprivation is indeed a pity!   One can never play Chopin beautifully enough, therefore never play his music too fast."

A brilliant illustration of how the master controls these rapidly moving harmonic masses, is afforded by the coda of the *F*-major Ballade.   (See Example 63.)

Observe that, with all freedom and boldness, the harmonic figures strike out into remote keys, but constantly return at a rhythmically vital moment. This indicates great technical adroitness. It is easy enough to abandon a key, but to return without compromising one's self is quite another matter. Note furthermore how the sequential elements are treated so as to avoid monotony. The first four-measure group is repeated an octave lower, followed by the passage *c* to *g*. Do not overlook the harmonic development of motive *c*. At *d* is a sequence one tone higher, then a contraction of it at *e*, in which the harmonic essence of it is preserved as thoroughly as if it were only a melodic figure. Again we see it growing shorter and shorter at *f* and *g*, running out into a pronounced return to the key of *A* minor.

Architecture has been frequently termed "frozen music," and if we may allow ourselves the complementary statement that music is "liquid architecture" we may be able to illustrate the difference between the classical and the Chopinesque music more clearly than by confining ourselves to purely musical terms. In Grecian architecture the masses of stone were so disposed that the chief pressure was vertical. The Romans introduced the arch as a feature of their structures, and from this germ was ultimately evolved the Gothic cathedral. Such an edifice, it is safe to assume, no Greek architect could attempt, inasmuch as it involved the construction of arches, domes, etc., with their side-thrusts at various angles, presenting problems for which, doubtless, the Hellenic builders had no solutions.* The melodic outlines and clear cut harmonies of the classical school of music may be said to bear a certain kinship to the chaste edifices of the Greeks. Indeed, we often hear a work of Haydn or Mozart compared to a Doric temple. With the introduction of themes that

---

*See Fergusson's "History of Architecture," Part I, Book II, Chapter V; Book III, Chapter I; Book IV, Chapter III.

imply the element of modulation, with motives that are virtually compound melodies, with members that have the character of harmonic designs, new principles are involved and new problems presented.

That such problems were likely to arise, was doubtless in a measure apprehended by Weber and Schubert, as witness the harmonic texture of the latter's *B*-minor Symphony. But the successful solution was reserved for a man coming from a land where multitudinous achievement had not yet induced satiety or discouragement. Sarmatia was to lighten through the strings in defiant originality, as Schumann might have expressed it. Far be it from me to intimate that Chopin had scheduled his modes of procedure. On the contrary, we know from the letters to his friend Titus Woyciechowski how hesitatingly Chopin expressed his opinion concerning the merits of his incipient *E*-minor Concerto. Possibly the modest, imaginative youth was so absorbed in the contemplation of the emotional side of his work (it embodied thoughts of his loved one), that he was scarcely aware of the intellectual significance of his undertaking. Helmholtz says, "The man of genius does at once, instinctively, what the scientists require years to explain." Wagner maintains that "composition is guesswork." True; but he might have added, "the man of genius solves the riddle, whereas the mere talent does not." That Chopin's prescience was equal to the problems presented him by the Fates, his works do abundantly testify.

XII

EMBELLISHMENTS

It is to Chopin we owe . . . the chromatic sinuosities of which
his pages offer such striking examples. *Franz Liszt.*
He loves decoration, but of that nobler kind under which poetic
ideality gleams more transparently. *Robert Schumann.*

In the evolution of all things, from the simpler organisms
to the higher types, from man's crudest efforts to his greatest
attainments, there appears along the line of progress first
that which is most essential, then the accessory members, and
finally the ornamentation. The seed, the root, the stalk,
stem, foliage and flower, outline the history of the plant.
The architect lays his foundations, then adds his walls, pil-
lars, beams, flooring, etc., and later the carvings and mural
decorations. The painter sketches his figures in outline, and
adds the details and coloring by degrees. Man first conquers
nouns and verbs, then little by little extends his mastery to
the other parts of speech. These suffice for the affairs of every
day, but when he attains the mental stature of a poet, he finds
that, in moments of exaltation, the most complete vocabulary
is inadequate to the expression of his emotions. Plain,
matter-of-fact statements are all too weak, so he resorts to
figures of speech. This is particularly true in the Orient,
where Nature stimulates the imagination to great activity.
Many a child has wondered, on reading the promise to
Abraham that his offspring should be in numbers "as the dust
of the earth," who could find elbow-room? Indeed, the difficulty of discriminating between statement and ornament, fact
and fancy, has throughout the ages occasioned strife, con-
tention, and merciless wars.

A similar metamorphosis is evident in the art of music.

Beginning with the monotonous chanting of the priests, the
Greeks slowly built up a series of tones which in the course

of a thousand years extended over a range of two octaves.* In the meantime instrumental music dissociated from vocal had developed to such a degree that the *aulos* virtuosos were able to execute a sort of symphonic poem, illustrating the conflict between Phœbus Apollo and the Python, in which numerous florid passages were introduced suggesting the writhings of the serpent. Effects of this sort may be heard in the performances of the Arabs on a kindred instrument, the *zamir*, where aside from glides, etc., the player often embellishes every note of a melody with a shake—the Oriental poetic hyperbole translated into tones.

The literature of our clavichord and harpsichord teems with ornamentation; we find a multitude of acciaccaturas and appoggiaturas, the bebung, doppelschlag, brechung, schleifer, mordents, double-mordents, pralltriller, turns, shakes, and what not, for which the old masters had elaborated such a complicated hieroglyphic outfit that skill and patience are needed for deciphering them now. But all these embellishments were not a luxury—they were, on the contrary, a necessity. When we try a passage from Bach or Rameau on a clavichord, we notice how the thin, delicate, evanescent tone requires reaffirmation.† Hence, if we are to produce tones

---

*Although the early lyre of the Greeks had four strings, giving the tetrachord, there had doubtless existed scales of two and three tones. Phonographic records of melodies of two tones as sung by the natives of certain islands in the Pacific are shown by Professor Stumpf of the Berlin University in his lectures; and Dr. Kane noted an Esquimau theme involving the use of three tones.

†One of the dreams of Wm. H. Sherwood was an improved pianoforte, provided with a means of sustaining a tone and producing a *crescendo* as well as a *diminuendo*. It so happened that he and I were among the first musicians to visit Mr. Edison at his laboratory and test his improved phonograph. It then occurred to Mr. Sherwood that possibly electricity might aid in solving the problem. The suggestion interested Mr. Edison, who told us he would see what he could do. He accordingly purchased a piano and began his experiments, but when we next called he had been seized with another idea, and abandoned the projected improvement, which was never perfected.

even suggestive of sustained whole notes, or even half-notes, these weird decorations, or something similar, must be called into requisition.

The embellishments which, with the classical masters, were compulsory, owing to physical conditions, became with Chopin also a necessity through his longing to beautify every musical phrase he employed. His fondness for Italian opera, together with his friendship for Bellini and others of that school, had an undoubted influence upon him. Realizing that of all instruments the human voice is the most beautiful, he could not fail to imitate the *bel canto* upon his own instrument. But Liszt calls especial attention to the difference between Chopin and those salon composers, with their servile imitation of the *fioriture* of the old school of Italian song; these became stereotyped and monotonous, whereas Chopin "imparted to these adornments the charm of novelty, surprise and variety, unsuited to the vocalist, but in perfect keeping with the character of his instrument." Attention has already been called to Liszt's appreciation of Chopin's extension of musical expression. In this connection he adds, "Chopin invented the admirable harmonic progressions which have given a serious character to his pages." These qualities may be discerned even in those apparently purely incidental decorative episodes.

The newly invented pedal was not only of great assistance in sustaining the tone of wires set in motion by striking a given key, but through the vibration of these strings in sympathy with others this tone would be still further prolonged. Thus, in Example 64, from the *Larghetto* of the *F*-minor

EXAMPLE 64

Concerto, it will be seen that the melodic note $B\flat$ is an over-tone of $E\flat$ in the bass, and that with each repetition of the tones $B\flat$ and $E\flat$ in the following chords the melodic tone will be reinforced. This swinging and swaying in mid-air of the harmonies is an outgrowth of the poetic Field nocturne-accompaniment. Indeed, von Bülow claims that Chopin modeled this concerto (in reality his first) upon that of Field in $A\flat$. A comparison of the two is truly profitable. Wagner says that no composer can be original at the outset, but Chopin came as near it as is possible. No one can study or even admire the work of another without being influenced thereby—to what extent, temperament, talent, and circumstances alone can determine. That Chopin was a student of Bach, Mozart, Beethoven, Hummel and Field is well known and sometimes obvious. But it was not long before the traits derived from those masters had become thoroughly absorbed and Chopinized.

In his preliminary studies for the F-minor Concerto he doubtless absorbed something of Field's mood, and the young Pole's opening theme is amusingly similar to a subordinate passage in D major in the first movement of the British master's above mentioned. But here all likeness ceases, for Chopin's theme rose in melodic freedom and harmonic richness, while Field's graceful phrase is unable to move outside of a circle, closing thrice on B, after which it escapes into a higher register. The *Larghetto* quoted gives an excellent idea of Chopin's embellishments in general. The tendency of the classical masters to present their *cantabile* themes (occasionally the more animated ones also) on each reappearance in ever-increasing richness, is shown in his treatment of the first subject. Compare the slow movements of Mozart's concertos in C major and C minor, also Beethoven's sonatas Op. 2, No. 1, and Op. 31, No. 1. It will be well to observe how this principle of ever-increasing enrichment is maintained throughout Chopin's career. One group of works will suffice to show this—the Nocturnes. See Nos. 1, 2, 3, 5, 8, 9, 11, 13, 15, 16, and especially those lovely poems, written at the close of his career, Nos. 17 and 18 (Op. 62).

Mozart and Beethoven usually play their arpeggios straight, clear-cut and to the point, although both masters occasionally indulge in chromatic changing-notes. Thus in the cadenzas of the first movements of the *C*-major and *C*-minor concertos, Mozart, in broken-chord passages, precedes the essential tones with semitone changing-notes. Beethoven naturally employs such more freely, while Weber seemed especially fond of strongly accented grace-notes before the tones of the broken chord. But nowhere do we find such peculiar employment of these accessory tones as in the more characteristic passages of Chopin, already seen in Examples 2, 13, 14, 15 and 16. The last mentioned, from the Polonaise in *E♭*, Op. 22, is doubtless one of the harshest, and to some students apparently the most gratuitously dissonant of Chopin's figures. But on inspection, what seems to be a series of dominant seventh-chords, with irrelevant tones thrust in, proves to be so many diminished seventh-chords with strongly marked changing-notes. How delicate and graceful this device can be rendered through dispersion may be seen in the delightful decorated arpeggio forming the cadenza

EXAMPLE 65

occurring in the seventh measure before the end of the Barcarolle, Op. 60. (See Example 65a.) Here we have to
deal with a chord of the augmented sixth and fifth, while the
bass sustains an organ-point on the tonic. (65b.)

The character of Chopin's figuration became more and
more differentiated from what was then in vogue; so much
so, in fact, that he was at that day seldom regarded as a
master of counterpoint. And yet his works are deeply imbued
with the spirit of that art. The method he employed might
be termed "decorated counterpoint." This sounds, indeed,
like painting the lily, and yet so gracefully did Chopin subdivide the tones of the diatonic scale, winding the weft of
melody in and out and around those paths usually taken by
writers of counterpoint, that this expression seems justified.

EXAMPLE 66

A glance at Example 66a from the Étude Op. 10, No. 4, will
show a fair specimen of the usual counterpoint, while Example 66b presents the inversion. By comparing them with
the original, the meaning of "decorated counterpoint" will
be obvious. It is furthermore evident that Chopin's music
is not by any means exclusively vertical, but very often, after
the manner of Bach and the later Beethoven, we find the
composer weaving his voices independently, but always with
reference to a beautiful sonority. See Berceuse, measures 7
to 14; the Barcarolle, introduction and much of the second
theme; the fourth Scherzo, in the passage after the second
section in *A♭,* beginning with the 17th measure after the
double-bar, then in the double rhythm (two *versus* three);
the Nocturne Op. 62, No. 2, throughout the second theme
and coda; etc.

Decorated organ-point was, up to Chopin's time, also something unknown, I believe. The example in the "working-out" division of the *A♭* Ballade has already been mentioned in Section X. Example 67 will show the beginning of the decorated organ-point with which Chopin leads his hearers to anticipate the return of the main theme of his *F*-major Ballade in the key of *A♭*. But no! After a graceful modulation we hear the pastoral theme in *F*,—the tonic, after all. This notion of deceiving the hearers concerning the reappearance of a theme was something of which Beethoven was very fond, but he never bewildered his audience quite in this way, nor with a constantly repeated scale as a decoration for his organ-point—another structural invention to the credit of Chopin.*

EXAMPLE 67

Still another novel invention was the reiteration of a set figure, above which was developed a melody or a series of phrases. An ingenious and effective procedure of this kind occurs in the Introduction to the Rondo, Op. 16, the most original moment in the entire work, by the way.† Bizet, in the Prelude of the first Suite from *l'Arlésienne*, has carried out this idea with remarkable skill. The clarinet plays a two-

---

*The elegiac chant of the wind-instruments superimposed upon the continually repeated descending scale, at the close of the first movement of Tschaikowsky's Pathetic Symphony, is a kindred device.   † See Ex. 68.

measure motive consisting of the notes $E\flat$, G, F and $E\flat$, while the violins sing a wholly independent melody, the harmonization constantly changing with charming result. The last movement ("Carillon") furnishes a yet more startling illustration. Horns, harp, etc., give the tones of the bells $G\sharp$, E, $F\sharp$ over and over again, wholly regardless of the brilliant themes intoned by the rest of the orchestra.

So variegated are many of Chopin's sequential designs, that they might well be termed "decorated sequences." We

EXAMPLE 68

have already quoted several in other connections. See Section III, Examples 14, 17; Section V, Examples 27, 31b, 34, 39b and e; Section XI, Example 63; Section XIII, Examples 82 and 83; Section XV, Examples 90, 91, 92 and 93.

The criticism might well be made that, according to the old and well-tried rule, the charmed number three, or at most four, ought not to be exceeded in the construction of sequences. We find that in several instances this limit has been overstepped. Were we to look for precedent it might readily be found in the works of Bach. (See Prelude to D-minor Toccata and other organ compositions where the element of phantasy prevails.) But an apology is needless, for we see that certain formations are merely embellishments of the diatonic scale. As a final instance, note the eight measures before the coda of the Rondo for two pianos, Op. 73. (See Example 69a.) Here we have three independent voices whirling about throughout three octaves, in a series of eleven groups. Aside from the charm of the ever-varying harmonic effect, the feeling is that of ornate scale-passages; and scales

pure and simple being recognized as orthodox and available,
they are all the more acceptable when thus treated. The
scale spirit is further emphasized in the coda of this Rondo
by two series of passages, where there is obviously no effort to
conceal its identity. (See Example 69b.)

EXAMPLE 69

That the traditional cadenzas belong to the order of embellishments, requires no comment, but those of Chopin are
so elaborately wrought as to acquire, in many instances, an
organic rather than a mere decorative character.

The ornamental character of the cadenza is so pronounced
that we are prone to regard it as something extraneous, even
lugged in for the sake of displaying the proficiency of the
performer. But when we find so conscientious an artist as
Chopin employing this feature so extensively, it surely must
have some higher mission than the gratification of personal
vanity. We have already seen how the master idealized and
beautified those technical figures which give the pianist an
opportunity to exhibit his powers, and in studying the cadenzas of Chopin we shall discern that same intense determi-
nation to avoid the commonplace, and the constant effort to
eliminate the ugly from everything he touched.

While a kinship exists between certain tonal and melodic
embellishments of Chopin and Mozart, there is rarely a
semblance of relationship in the cadenzas. Once in a great
while a simple scale reminds one of the classical masters, but

little else.   When Beethoven treated the cadenza, he sometimes gave it a thematic coloring.   (See the Sonata in *C*, Op.
2, No. 2, coda.)   Occasionally Chopin does the same.   The
last pages of the Barcarolle afford illustrations of two types;
first, the decorated arpeggio above given (Example 65), then
another, derived from a figure which gives it a thematic import.   Beginning at Tempo I°, the coda is formed from the
imitative portion of his second subject.   Upon a tonic organ-
point a series of weirdly beautiful sequences is formed in
which the vital feature is the imitation between soprano and
alto derived from the second theme (in *A* major).   Ever
steadily advancing, with intermittent retrogressions, the wave
of tone breaks in this cadenza, receding till the refrain from
the main theme recurs.   The organ-point continues, but after
the previous bold chromatic passages the contrast afforded by
diatonic harmonies is very graceful.   A new figure in thirty-
second-notes brings us to a closing cadenza evolved from this
figure, which by degrees swells from *pianissimo* to *fortissimo*.
Another specimen in which the relationship between the figure
in the main body of the work, and the cadenza which is an
outgrowth of the same, is to be found, is the *E♭-major* Polonaise Op. 22.

EXAMPLE 70

The strength and unity afforded by giving the cadenza a
thematic character was felt by the older masters, as may be
seen in their concertos, and more recent composers have skill-
fully welded them into the body of the work so that this
unity is greatly increased.   Witness those of Schumann, Grieg

and Tschaikowsky—the latter, particularly, assumes symphonic proportions. Even in the symphony there are moments where through exuberance of feeling (Schumann's in *B♭*, last movement) a pause, as if in contemplation (Beethoven's in *C* minor, first movement), a purely sincere and emotional cadenza is indulged in. This shows that the cadenza may be the means of expressing a dramatic idea or intensifying a situation.

Thus far the cadenza has been considered only in its relationship to absolute music. It would be strange if that which is available in music *per se* dissociated from other arts, would not prove useful when combined with poetry and the drama. So indeed is the case with cadenzas. We find them in vocal music as a natural means of elaborating the close of a song or aria, and this not merely in the works of Italians, but of serious Germans like Beethoven, Schubert and Schumann. They are naturally introduced to display the vocal virtuosity of the singer, as we see in countless operas. Sometimes they are accompanied with solo instruments, as in the great *Lucia* aria for soprano (flute assisting), or the bass solo in Act V of the *Huguenots,* with bass clarinet as the sole accompaniment.

While in the majority of cases they are musically meaningless, merely serving for external display, certain composers have added a true thematic interest to these vocalizations. Excellent specimens are the Polonaise in *Mignon* by Thomas, and the "Bell Aria" in *Lakmé* by Delibes. By this means the character of these otherwise extraneous fragments is elevated to the dignity of true architectural art. But there are moments when the spirit of the cadenza may be justifiably summoned, as we have seen in instrumental music; namely, where the dramatic situation requires a prolongation of *the element of suspense.*

The closing scene of *Die Walküre* shows us Brünnhilde surrounded by flames which can be penetrated only by him who knows no fear. Who this hero is to be, the orchestra tells us—Siegfried. During the first two and a half acts of the ensuing drama, *Siegfried,* we behold with ever tenser interest the valiant youth forging his sword, slaying the dragon, appropriating the fatal Ring, following the bird, disputing the way with Wotan the Wanderer, and at last we are brought to the "Walkürenfels," where still sleeps the heroine. The master's sense of proportion forbids that the hero be seen at once, or that he shall enter with unseemly haste, and yet we must know something of his whereabouts and intentions. At this instant the element of suspense must be emphasized, something which Wagner effects by means of a cadenza—a cadenza of heroic proportions, the most remarkable ever known. Beginning with a development of the bewitching theme associated with Freia, the Goddess of Love, the first violins make that unheard-of sweep from low *G* (open string) to the uttermost limits of the upper regions. The trombones whisper the theme of Fate, and the violins descend from *C♯* in altissimo with the slumber-motive of Brünnhilde. Siegfried enters, and after contemplating the motionless figure with awe and wonder, cuts the cords, releasing his future bride from the armour which she shall no longer wear. This, too, is a moment of deep import and not to be lightly passed over. With new phases of the Sword-theme (horns, then clarinets) a secondary cadenza is evolved, thus intensifying the significance of the event. Indeed, the entire action from the rise of the curtain to the awakening of Brünnhilde might be regarded as an elaborate cadenza preceding the reprise. The dramatic phase of the reprise is the return of Brünnhilde to life, the joy of which is intensified by the hitherto untasted delights of human love.

After this, who shall speak slightingly of the element of ornamentation, when justified by æsthetic necessity and idealized by men of genius like Chopin and Wagner?

XIII

ORCHESTRAL EXPERIMENTS

Neither do men put new wine into old bottles: else the bottles
break, and the wine runneth out and the bottles perish.

Matthew ix: 17.

The architects of antiquity, in planning their earliest stone
structures, copied many details from their buildings of wood.
Naïve as this procedure may seem, it is merely in accordance
with the axiom affirming that all progress is from the known
to the unknown. Unconsciously yielding to this tendency, the
pioneers of orchestration patterned their scores after their
choral works; indeed, in many instances, the instrumentation
was a mere duplication of the several vocal parts. When we
compare the piano compositions of Mozart and Beethoven
with their symphonies, a similar kinship is evident. In the
light of these precedents, the thoughtful student might anticipate in the orchestration of Chopin a richness of harmonic
texture such as characterizes the composer's pianoforte literature; but should he cherish such expectations, he is doomed to
disappointment. On inspecting those works in which Chopin
summons the orchestra to his assistance we frequently detect
a striking difference between the quality of the music assigned
to the pianoforte and that allotted to the orchestra.

How shall we account for this discrepancy?

Is it possible that the composer of the Études, with all their
unusual harmonic and structural beauty, was incapable of
writing the music of a symphony worthy to rank with the
achievements of the classical period? Shall we assume that
the magician who cast such a spell over the keyboard was
unable to exercise his necromancy upon the instruments of
the orchestra? When hundreds of musicians, who make no
claims to creative gifts, acquire with comparative ease the
requisite routine, is it credible that the genius of Chopin was
inadequate to the task of inditing a symphonic score?

Before casting the ballots which shall decide the fate of this remarkable candidate for orchestral honors, it will be advisable to pause a moment in order to consider the condition of the orchestra for which Chopin composed. Attention has already been directed to the powerful incentive afforded his imagination by the improvement of the pianoforte. The question at once presents itself, "Had the mechanism of the orchestra been developed to such a degree of perfection as to stimulate his creative faculties to an equal extent?" The answer comes at once, and with significant emphasis :—"No !"

The foundation of every orchestra is the string-group, which is capable of rendering a homogeneous chromatic scale from the lowest register to the highest. Now, although this valued band of instruments had long since attained such perfection that makers of to-day are happy to create the counterpart of an Amati, a Guarnerius, or a Stradivarius, the phenomenal extension of violin-technique introduced by Paganini had not yet become common property. The orchestral violinists of Chopin's day were not qualified to play such figures as embellish the score of the "Magic Fire Scene," nor were the viola-players equal to the demands of the *Tannhäuser* overture or the "Ride of the Valkyries." This orchestral virtuosity, which complements the pianistic achievements of Chopin and Liszt, is something of comparatively recent date.* Furthermore, in the early decades of the nineteenth century the violins rarely ascended beyond the fifth position (highest tone f^3), until Beethoven took them to the c above (*Egmont* overture) ; and since then Wagner has soared to still loftier altitudes.

If such limitations hampered the composers for the strings, those who employed the wind-instruments were annoyed by far more serious restrictions. The so-called "wood-wind

---

*The late Wilhelmj, who was first *concertmeister* at Bayreuth in 1876, when recounting to a friend of mine his experiences on this occasion, mentioned sitting up night after night studying the intricacies of his part.

choir" possessed a compass similar to that of the strings—even greater if piccolo and double-bassoon be included. Throughout this entire range a chromatic scale was indeed feasible, but the number of trills and other embellishments that were difficult or quite impossible to execute clogged the flow of melody. Even when a phrase was practicable in one key, its repetition in another desirable tonality was out of the question, thus confining the composer to a meagre assortment of scales which soon became hackneyed if great ingenuity were not exercised. Moreover, the old instruments were frequently defective in intonation; in fact, before the distribution of the apertures had been scientifically regulated, the deviation from pitch of certain tones was hopelessly chronic.

Surely, to a man of Chopin's extraordinary refinement of taste and feeling, this prospect could not have been inviting. By comparing the tables of forbidden trills, etc., in the treatise on instrumentation by Berlioz (original edition) with these same tables as revised by Strauss,* we gain some idea of the enormous improvements in mechanism and tone-quality, as well as extension of compass, in the flute, oboe, clarinet and bassoon, thanks to Böhm and kindred inventors.

But if the wood-wind presented such difficulties to the composer of the early romantic school, what shall we say of the brass department? Of this group, the only members admitted to the symphonic circle were the trumpets and horns—instruments originally associated with war and the chase, but which in time had became sufficiently civilized and refined to render them eligible to indoor activity. Nevertheless, as they possessed the strongest voices of the orchestral assemblage, with small incitement they betrayed their barbaric origin. Coincident with these stentorian qualities was a very rudimentary vocabulary, including neither the chromatic nor

---

*See the Strauss-Berlioz "Orchestration" (2 Vols. Edition Peters, Leipzig, 1905.)

even the diatonic scale, being confined to the tones produced by "overblowing," which gives the series shown below.

EXAMPLE 71

In the time of Bach and Händel all these tones, from the second up to the sixteenth, and even higher, were employed in spite of the dissonant character of tones 7, 11, 13, and 14, which do not correspond with the notes that are here employed to indicate them. The horn-player, by inserting his hand in the bell of his instrument, could rectify the intonation in some cases, and even produce other tones by this method of "stopping," but none had the clarity and richness of the open tones.* Discarding the discordant tones 7, 11, 13, and 14, we have the material for three chords (see Example 72 *a, b* and *c*) ; the first two, tonic and dominant, are the most important in our musical system, the boundaries, as it were, of all musical expression. During the period of the classical

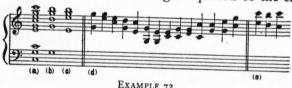

(a) (b) (c)   (d)   (e)

EXAMPLE 72

symphony, the performers rarely ever touched the upper tones given at *e*. The principal harmonies at the command of trumpet and horn-players were the formulas given in Example 72 at *d,* which demonstrate the persistence of tonic and dominant. As above intimated, the brass executants were prone to make their presence felt, and as they laid chief stress on these primary harmonies, the more refined and yielding instruments were drawn into the irresistible vortex of tone

---

*Gevaert's method of indicating by means of black notes those tones which do not correspond with any in our European systems of scales is here adopted.

which centered in *Tonic and Dominant*. One of the great difficulties in the classical period was to obviate the tendency of the brass to obliterate the melodic designs by giving too forcible utterance to middle parts, often mere *Füllstimmen* (padding). Even at the present day, when the strings in many orchestras have outweighed the wood, some *forte* passages in the classical symphonies are so strongly seasoned with brass and percussion that the more delicate melodic and sometimes even the harmonic flavor is wholly lost.

The reader will doubtless recall the finale of Beethoven's *A*-major Symphony, where there is a regrettable inability of the brass to finish the melodic phrase conceived by the composer. I endeavor to suggest by means of large and small notes the relative strength of the different parts.

EXAMPLE 73

Where it was possible for the brass to give the exact theme, well and good; but when the break occurs, and the brass goes one way, strings and wood-wind another, the effect is unsatisfactory. More than this, the old trumpets were unable to proceed in octaves to the *e* and *e*¹, so the upper *e* was doubled by the second trumpet, placing undue emphasis on the higher tone, which is strident enough as it stands.

On account of the rudimentary brass, not only were melodies mutilated at times almost beyond recognition, but rhythmic values were frequently weirdly distorted. Take, for instance, the following bit from the Scherzo of the same symphony.

For the reason that trumpets and kettledrums could yield
the *f*'s and *a*'s of the *F*-major chord, the first three measures
were played *fortissimo*.   The   fourth   measure   contains   a
dominant seventh-chord; but as this was inaccessible to these
instruments, the horns were left alone, giving the *C* which is
common to both chords.   In the next four measures the proc-
ess was reversed, the first three being light and the fourth
heavy.   In the eight measures following a similar discrepancy
occurs, and for similar reasons the third measure in one group
of four measures is accented, while the fourth of the succeeding group is emphasized.

EXAMPLE 74

When Beethoven brought in the main theme of the initial
movement of the Fifth Symphony announcing the reprise, he
undoubtedly longed to give out those gigantic thunder-knocks
with full orchestra in octaves, but owing to the nature of the

EXAMPLE 75

brass, he was obliged to effect a compromise, with the result here shown. (See Example 75.)

In the finale of the same work he was more successful in making the strong voices give out his theme, although, as may be seen in Example 76, they failed him in the seventh measure, so that even the subdominant chord is but meagrely sketched.*

EXAMPLE 76

Considering Chopin's genius for rich tone-combinations and bold modulations, it is not strange that this number failed to arouse his enthusiasm, inasmuch as the principal theme, based on trumpet formulas, moves seldom, and not far from the tonic. On the other hand, "The Death of Siegfried" would unquestionably have rejoiced his soul. Wagner's tone-poem possesses qualities equally heroic, while the fanfares it embodies are conceived for the improved chromatic brass, which permit a range of key and a wealth of harmony wholly impossible to the instruments for which Beethoven wrote. The trombones, with their noble voices and perfect chromatic scale, equally effective in *piano* and *forte* throughout the compass of tenor and bass, were, indeed, at Beethoven's dis-

---

*Furthermore, this chord was out of tune, as the *f* is one of the discordant tones—always too flat on the "natural" trumpets and horns.

posal. But he introduced them in this finale for the first time in the history of the symphony, and even then treated them simply like more vigorous horns, the formulas he gives them being practically the same, with now and then an extraneous note (see *F* in bass clef of Example 76). Beethoven availed himself rarely of their wonderful *pianissimo* (see the Prison Scene in *Fidelio*), and scarcely tested their chromatic qualities. In this respect he was surpassed by Schubert, who employed a larger harmonic lexicon, and whose prophetic eye beheld new orchestral possibilities.

In his scintillating series of studies in the Chopinesque piano literature, James Huneker refers to my "potent brief in behalf of the original orchestration of the *E*-minor Concerto." I myself cannot exactly place this "brief," but the author doubtless had in mind my essay* on "Schumann and the Modern Orchestration," wherein I called attention to the fact that both Schumann and Chopin were confronted by a great problem. This problem concerned *the expression of romantic ideas through the medium of the classical orchestra.*

Possibly the history of art affords no more striking instance of the futility of putting new wine into old bottles to the consequent detriment of both.

Having shown the inadequacy of the rococo orchestra to the demands of Beethoven when he sought to spread his wings for freer flight, it is easy to indicate the absurdity of attempting to shackle the Muse of Chopin with this defective mechanism. Let us see how some of his more characteristic pieces would look arranged for modern orchestra. We must select of course such as are not indissolubly wedded to specifically pianistic figures.

Several of the Preludes from Op. 28 permit other settings. Thus, No. 4 might be performed by clarinet, oboe and horns. No. 6 might be rendered by a similar group of instruments,

---

*Published in Philip Hale's "Musical Record," Boston, Nov. and Dec., 1898.

with perhaps a bassoon added for variety. No. 9 would be feasible for horn-quartet and tuba;* better, of course, if varied by the addition of trumpets and trombones. No. 20 could be easily performed by the complete brass group; while No. 21 is scarcely less practicable for the lighter brass, adding flutes, oboes and clarinets to extend the compass upwards. With flutes, clarinets and horns the entire Étude in E♭, Op. 10, No. 11, might be given in its full harmonic integrity, although the arpeggio and other pianistic effects would be missing.

All this seems quite a matter of course to the concert-goer and opera habitué of the twentieth century. But on the day that Chopin penned the mysterious, impalpable harmonies of the E♭-minor Étude (Op. 10, No. 6), what man would have dared think of transferring it to the brass group of the orchestra? Not even Berlioz himself, in his wildest enthusiasm, would have been so audacious. But, by one of those coincidences which render fact sometimes more startling than fiction, within a few months of the inception of this Étude† the valve-horn came into use,‡ and this invention rendered just such elaborate harmonic structures accessible to the brass-wind. Hence, as we have already seen, Wagner enriched the quality of orchestral music through the employment of this device, and the scores of *Tristan und Isolde* and the *Ring* furnish many a page embellished with music to be voiced by trumpets, horns and tubas, of as complex texture as this ethereal Étude.

Lest the reader infer that I endorse the arrangement of Chopin's works for orchestra (as Mme. George Sand claimed

---

*The trills in measures 3 and 4 would be clumsy.

†In his "Handbook to Chopin's Works" Mr. G. C. Ashton Johnson gives the dates 1829-31 as marking the period in which the Études Op. 10 were composed.

‡F. A. Gevaert, in his "Neue Instrumentenlehre," states that in 1830 the valve-horns were introduced.

they would be, in time), I must, on the contrary, add my testimony to that of the many who do not care for such metamorphoses.* The Funeral March from Op. 35 is doubtless the most effective, although the *fortissimo* of the Theodore Thomas version was somewhat brutal. Even Carl Müller-Berghaus, who won such renown through his masterly transcriptions of Liszt's Hungarian Rhapsodies, was unsuccessful in his treatment of Chopin's Polonaise Op. 53, many measures of which sound as though the bottom had dropped out, there being nothing to compensate for the absence of that rich flood of overtones engendered by well-distributed harmonies, assisted by the damper-pedal of the pianoforte.

An apology for suggesting possible arrangements of the various numbers may be found in the fact that by this means the difference between the harmonic and structural qualities of the music of Chopin and that of his predecessors will stand out more vividly. This difference will be accentuated if the assumed arrangements of the Chopin numbers for brass be compared with the trumpet and horn parts in the slow movements of Mozart, Haydn and Beethoven. In many cases the melodies are obviously nothing more nor less than horn or trumpet formulas. That the classical masters gave such great variety to themes made to fit the very limited capacity of these instruments, is a source of wonder. But it would be vastly more astonishing had Chopin, with all his wealth of harmonic themes, been able to use a single one of them—had he given it to the brass without its being cramped, crippled, and distorted beyond recognition.

This brings us once more for an instant to the consideration of Chopin's much discussed unsatisfactory work in the classical forms. That some of his sonata-themes are less

---

*It is not within the scope of this essay to consider the transcriptions of Chopin's works for other instruments or their rearrangements for pianoforte, interesting as some of them are. The fact that such exist, however, shows the vitality of the thought in the originals.

striking and original than those of many of his Ballades, Scherzos, Études, etc., is self-evident, but it is only when compared with these other works of the artist that they appear weak or uninspired. Chopin was not the only composer who seemed to be obsessed with the idea that, just as the fugue-subject must comply with a long series of limitations before it is fugue-worthy, so must a sonata-theme conform to certain requirements respecting shape and size. This explains why Chopin, when writing in the specifically classical forms, employed themes that are classical rather than Chopinesque, melodic rather than harmonic; which may be easily grasped by the hands with little or no extension, and which, in their development, run along the old highway instead of in the new, bold path he had blazed in the Romantic forest. We feel this in the first attempt, Sonata Op. 4, in the Trio Op. 8, the Sonata for Piano and 'Cello Op. 65, and in the *Allegro de Concert* Op. 46, where we hardly recognize the real Chopin until he has put some eighty or ninety measures between himself and the classical beginning. Thence onward he breathes more freely. With ever-growing confidence he asserts his powers; the harmonies increase in richness until, as shown in Section V, they assume Wagnerian contours.

Even in the more mature Sonata Op. 58 we are conscious, in the first few measures, of classical influence, but the composer soon frees himself. In the Sonata in $B\flat$ minor, Op. 35, we find no lingering survivals of the classical sonata-themes, although throughout the entire work the spirit of that form is manifest.

That Chopin was a master of those elements which contribute to the making of a sonata is possibly evident from what has been said here and previously (see Sections VIII and X). What concerns us at this point is the fact that the classical influences which affected the shape of certain themes also affected those of his concerted numbers, at least when the orchestra was involved, paralyzing in a measure his creative

faculties.   We need but compare the first entries of those
themes that are shaved down to the requirements of the
classical orchestra, with their subsequent enrichment when
given to the piano.   Incidentally be it said, that the long introductory *tutti* to the *E*-minor Concerto, so often alluded to
as a defect in Chopin's style, was merely due to classical precedent, the demands of tradition being that all the themes of the
concertos should be rehearsed before the entrance of the solo
instrument, which, like the theatrical star, must be long looked
for with eager expectancy.

Chopin's pianistic creations of this early period already
evince a pronounced style, a term which cannot be applied to
his contemporaneous orchestral work.   The Don Juan Variations Op. 2, the Fantaisie on Polish Airs Op. 13, and the
Krakowiak Op. 14, were scored the same year, 1828.   As
the last-named contains more individual expression and a
smaller proportion of adopted themes than the others, and
(what is more to our purpose) has not been re-orchestrated
like the concertos and the Polonaise Op. 22, we can get a
glimpse of the orchestral world as it seemed to Chopin.   In
the Krakowiak, pianoforte and orchestra are much more in-
terdependent than is generally supposed.   Indeed, the main
body of the work is fraught with thematic allusion,* frequently in the augmentation.   This is all the more remarkable,
as the harmonic designs outlined by the piano passages are
often so involved that they seem to preclude the employment
of melodic figures.   Sometimes we find a fragment of exact
imitation, as in the closing measures of the Andantino of the
introduction (pianoforte and clarinet), also in the last measures on page 9 of the orchestral score (bassoon and oboe),
and on pages 15 and 16 (clarinet and bassoon).   Among
structural crudities may be mentioned those reminiscences

---

*So insistent is this allusion, that it seems almost to be the result of
pedagogical admonitions; as is the case with the Sonata in *C* minor, which
also dates from the year 1828.

which might have been rendered truer to the theme (see the solo bits for clarinet and flute on pages 23 and 24. These might easily have taken on the form of the ensuing oboe phrase, thus strengthening the impression of the quotation from the main theme and affording a greater contrast with the fragments of the secondary theme which are given to bassoon and horn.*

Again, in some of the references to this or that feature of the leading themes, Chopin does not always finish the phrase in the same tone-color. In other words, a quotation begun by one instrument is concluded by another, sometimes even in a different register, a procedure quite out of keeping with good orchestral syntax. For instance, on page 27, measures 1–5, the third and fourth measures of the main theme appear in augmentation. The flute begins the phrase, but, in order to avoid parallel octaves with the bass, the melody is given an upward twist while the bassoon completes it an octave below. Now, the passage would be more satisfactory if the flute (better yet if taken in this register by the oboe) had been given the entire phrase, and the bass progression altered to E, $B\natural$, C, $G\sharp$, A—or, if this should spoil the piano figures, the melody itself might be slightly altered as the composer has so frequently done elsewhere. A similar procedure occurs in measures 9-13, page 28, involving clarinet and oboe; again on page 28, measures 1-4 (flute and oboe).

But in spite of occasional discrepancies, which merely indicate lack of experience, we find evidence of true instinct for genuine thematic work. Observe how artistically Chopin arranges the dying-out of the piano figure in the first measures of page 29. Here flute and clarinet sustain in octaves the tones a^1 and a^2, then imitate in double augmentation the last notes of the piano phrase, in turn taken up by the bassoon and once more by the pianoforte in the lowest register. This

---

*Breitkopf & Härtel, "Erste kritisch durchgesehene Gesammtausgabe."

is after the manner of Beethoven, and akin to the close of the working-out division in the *B♭*-minor Scherzo Op. 31. (See Section X, Example 57.)

Concerning the orchestration proper, the score of the Krakowiak presents an aspect typically classical: twofold woodwind, horns, trumpets, kettledrums, pianoforte and strings.

With reference to Chopin's treatment of the instruments, the most noticeable features are as follows. The flutes are employed *unisono* in all the *tuttis*. This is less commendable than the conventional method of dividing them, at least occasionally. The string accompaniments are at times too light for the piano part, especially when marked *pp* and *morendo,* as on page 11, while the doubling of the wind-instruments on a single part, as we see on the same page (clarinet and horn—later clarinet and bassoon), is seldom advisable.

On the other hand, the treatment of the string-group is in the main excellent; the open strings and double-stops are pretty thoroughly utilized. The introductory passage for pianoforte with the eight- and two-foot tone, accompanied by widely dispersed strings, is charming. Piquant and sparkling, too, is the presentation of the secondary theme (in *D* minor), the melody given in octaves by the pianoforte *legato-staccato,* the accompaniment in the strings *pizzicato.*

Chopin elsewhere manifests a talent for effective orchestral combinations and unusual devices. Unconsciously following Schubert (whose symphonies no one had then heard), Chopin extended the range of the brass (as well as its powers of expression) by adding a trombone to the score of his *E*-minor Concerto—an unheard-of procedure in concerted music. He also used two pairs of horns and *three* kettledrums. In the finale of the *F*-minor Concerto he introduced a most daring figure for the old horns,* as shown in Example 77a. A more

---

*Here the player has to skip one of the series of open tones in rapid movement.

conventional fanfare is given at b. The Larghetto in the
F-minor Concerto contains a dramatic recitative for the piano,
while the strings add a sinister tremolo, an effect which Liszt
elaborates to such good purpose in his massive *E♭* Concerto.
Again, one should not overlook the exhilarating second theme

EXAMPLE 77

of the Rondo of the *E*-minor concerto, given by the piano in
octaves while the strings urge it on with its propulsive Slavic
rhythm; nor should we forget the excellent thematic development in the opening movement of this same work;—observe
the treatment of the main theme in measures 27 to 60; note
especially the bass progressions.

This certainly justifies the assertion that Chopin as well as
the other great masters had a certain prophetic vision concerning what might be done with the orchestra. Composing
for the pianoforte with an insight into its proper treatment,
also belongs to the art of instrumentation. Surely, he who
could so thoroughly apprehend, utilize, idealize and exhaust
the resources of the pianoforte, must have felt that kindred
potentialities lay latent in the orchestra. It is truly tantaliz-
ing to think that he was a contemporary of Paganini, Böhm
and Sax, who were so wonderfully extending the expressive
powers of the strings, wood-wind and brass. But long before
their inventions and discoveries were generally applied, Chopin had wisely abandoned the idea of laboring with an inadequate orchestral medium, and confined his activity to the
pianoforte.

This was but another proof of his genius. The mission
to which he had been assigned was the widening of the musical
horizon, and the only possible medium was the pianoforte.

XIV

UNIVERSALITY

A pupil should not be kept too long at the study of one method, or confined to the taste of one nation. What is truly beautiful must not be imitated, but felt, and assimilated with the individual genius. We must not take one man, or one nation, as a model, for these only afford examples more or less imperfect.

Joseph Elsner [*in letter to Chopin*].

Time was when the term catholic applied to all orthodox Christian believers. At the present day, convention has so narrowed its meaning, that it is popularly employed to designate only those of the Roman confession.

So powerful is the voice of music, so appealing its message, so direct its address to peoples of divers tongues, that it is sometimes called a universal language. No wonder, then, that compositions are frequently esteemed in direct proportion to their universality. Doubtless composers of all nations should be eligible to the creation of works to which the coveted adjective *universal* may be applied, but its use has become so restricted of late that its employment now generally refers to music made in Germany.* Not long since I was discussing the structural character of Chopin's creations with one of Germany's ablest composers, a man of broad sympathies and widely comprehensive views. I called his attention to Chopin's novel devices, logical development and consequential interweavings of inner voices. Admitting, of course, their undeniable beauty, he did not grow so warm over the workmanship, adding that the works of Herr X. were *"universeller."* Now, this Herr X. was born on German soil, but his inspiration is often called in question, though none

---

*This usage is not peculiar to Germany, nor does it indicate chauvinistic sentiment in that country. On the contrary, nowhere else does the theatre possess such a rich, international repertory, while the concert stage is hardly less cosmopolitan.

doubts his technical proficiency.   Universal!   One sometimes
grows weary of the specification.   It most assuredly does not
comprehend all desirable qualities.   When we hear that this
or that "all-around" or general-utility composer is more universal than Chopin, we are tempted to reply, "Yes, truly, so
are weeds more universal than roses, and sparrows than night-
ingales."

Whenever a creative mind shows such power that its imprint is seen upon the works of artists in foreign lands employing other idioms and different mechanical media from
its own, we may safely assume that this indicates the possession
of qualities other than those purely local and national.   Thus,
the success of Chopin in the idealization of Polish folk-music
gave the impetus to the creation of such works as Liszt's Hungarian Rhapsodies, Dvořák's "Slavic Dances," and that
brilliant array of compositions by Grieg and the great Russians in which the melodies of their respective countryfolk
were exploited.   This influence, however, is merely external,
although in many (possibly most) cases, Chopinesque textural
traits are in evidence.   Bizet's *Djamileh, l'Arlésienne* and
Carmen betray a fondness for folk-songs conceived in quaint
modes and Oriental scales, with glowing harmonies and rich
thematic work, which point unmistakably toward Chopin;
indeed, certain highly elaborated cadence-formulas and other
details are directly derived.   This is also true of Delibes in
his *Lakmé,* which evinces similar refinement in the treatment
of exotic material.

The influence upon German composers, Schumann, Wagner, etc., has already been referred to.   An editorial comment in the London "Musical Record" of March, 1910, is
to the point: "No composer ever intentionally took him as
a model, but Chopin exerted a strong influence over those who
came after him, notably over Wagner.   Reminiscence-hunters
are not unjustly looked upon with disfavor, but in this case
no hunting is required—the reminiscences stare one, as it

were, in the face. Actual note resemblances, however curious,
are mere accidents; the chromatic element it must surely have
been which so attracted Wagner." The writer evidently
feels the power of Chopin's harmonic masses and his logical
development of them, and notes that similar material and
similar workmanship are manifested in the best of Wagner's
tone-structures.

Let the reader but pause for an instant and imagine how
Siegfried and *Götterdämmerung* would sound if the composer had employed no other harmonic material than that
which we find in Mozart or Beethoven at their best; let us
say, such as we find in the former's G-minor Symphony (first
movement) or the latter's Sonata Op. 57 ("Appassionata").
There would be much missing. On the other hand, let him
fancy that he has never heard anything either of Chopin or
Wagner; then that the action of the Trilogy be filled with a
magic fluid which contains the essence of certain Chopinesque
pieces like the études Op. 10, Nos. 4, 6, 7, 9, 11 and 12; Op.
25, Nos. 1, 2, 3, 6, 7, 9, 10 (first theme), 11 and 12; the
preludes Op. 28, Nos. 1, 2, 4, 6, 8, 11, 12, 14, 16, 17, 18,
19, 21, 22, 24, and Op. 45, together with the sonata in B♭
minor, especially the working-out section of the first movement, with its premonishment of the "Götterdämmerung" motive, and the second part of the scherzo with its prophecy of
the "Feuerzauber." Here the aforementioned lack of the
harmonic element is by no means so pronounced as in the
former hypothetical case. On comparing this with the version by Wagner himself, the result would prove truly interesting. Wagner's would show at times greater power, and
reveal his extraordinary capacity for the absorption and
further elaborations of those principles first applied by Chopin. At the same time, it would not always give evidence of
the rare refinement of the Pole, or testify to that unusual
gift for preserving the balance of power among conflicting
tonalities which characterized Chopin's art.

Among the many features that might be cited, wherein Chopin showed himself to be a stimulating influence affecting his colleagues and successors, we may mention his original manner of delaying the resolutions of dissonant chords, suspensions and changing-notes.

In Example 78a (from Op. 10, No. 1) we see the suspension *C* on the first beat of the first measure not only delayed, but resolved four octaves below by *B* on the fourth beat; also a similar procedure in the sequence two measures later. But far more remarkable is the passage from Op. 10, No. 7, shown in Example 78b, where the suspended tone *F* in the middle voice (second beat, first measure) is not resolved until two measures have intervened. This illustrates admirably the tendency of the ear to retain a dissonant tone, with the expectation of a resolution at a moment rhythmically marked.

EXAMPLE 78

Wagner employs this device frequently, possibly nowhere with more marked dramatic force than in *Tristan und Isolde,* where the unhappy pair partake of the love-potion. The theme of Desire (or Love-Charm) bursts forth from the entire orchestra in the strongest accents, covering a range of

five octaves.   But stormy passages of the strings descending
two octaves from high $E\natural$ precede the resolution of the dissonant intervals which occurs in the medium register.   (See
Example 79.)

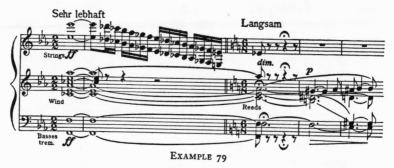

EXAMPLE 79

In Chopin's Nocturne Op. 62, No. 1, we have a delayed
changing-note of peculiarly cutting character, as it comes before the third of the chord. (See Example 80.)   A curious
parallel occurs in King Mark's theme (*Tristan und Isolde,*
close of Act II).   It is interesting to see how the feature at
N. B. 1 is amplified by Wagner, at N. B. 2, and how delicately
the non-resolution of the $G\natural$ at N. B. 3 renders this expressive theme perfect of its kind.

EXAMPLE 80

The prolongation of the cadence-formula is sometimes pro-
ductive of very artistic effects.   The opening of the *G*-minor
Ballade seems on first acquaintance to be in the key of *A*♭
major.   It is simply the first inversion of the chord of the
second degree of *G* minor with the fundamental lowered
(the so-called Neapolitan sixth).   This introduction is noth-

ing more nor less than a wonderfully idealized cadence-formula. (See Example 81a.) The same principles are applied (although with wholly different harmonies) in the Prelude to Act II of *Tristan und Isolde.* Critics attacked Wagner for thus plunging into a sea of unprepared, unresolved dissonance, but on analysis we find the outline is quite as refined and as thoroughly consistent with the laws of harmony as was Chopin's, just quoted, only it takes him twenty-seven measures to reach the tonic triad in its fundamental position. (See Example 81b.)

EXAMPLE 81

These unusual quickenings and delayings of the modulatory and other harmonic processes are allied to the treatment of the fugue-theme in diminution and augmentation; devices of the polyphonic period. Be it remarked in passing, that here, too, it is more difficult to treat a moving harmonic mass in this manner than when we are dealing with only one or two voices. Compare, for instance, the passages shown in Ex-

EXAMPLE 82

EXAMPLE 83

amples 82 and 84 with Bach's Fugue in *C* minor, in the second volume of the Well-Tempered Clavichord, and the one in *C♯* major that follows.

EXAMPLE 84

Chopin's daring experiment, already made in his first sonata, of running together a series of chords of the sixth in chromatic succession, is doubtless referable to the progression of the above-mentioned "Neapolitan sixth" chord to the first inversion of the major tonic triad.   (See Example 85a.)

EXAMPLE 85

One need only try a sequence based upon this progression, and the thing is accomplished.   (See Example 85b.)   The descending series in Chopin's first sonata was followed by ascending series in the *E*-minor Concerto, carefully kept with-

EXAMPLE 86

in key-bounds.* (See Section X, Example 56b.) In the Polonaise Op. 53 we find it introduced in a more daring manner;
something like the treatment employed at the close of the
one in E♭ major, Op. 22, also in the scherzo of the Sonata
Op. 35. (See Example 86.)

How vividly Wagner saw the possibilities of this device, is
suggested by the quotations from the last act of *Die Walküre*.
At one time it lends its invaluable aid in simulating the wind
as it bears the Wish-Maidens on the storm-cloud. (See Example 87.)

EXAMPLE 87

Again it mingles with a fiercer element—fire, the visible
symbol of Loge's approach. (See Example 88.) Observe
how manifold are the master's means of moulding this plastic
material; now in descending gusts; now in triple trills, suggesting flickering flames; again in zig-zags of open fifths.
Truly, Wagner had studied his Chopin to good advantage!

The consecutive chords of the sixth, with their manifold
variants, shown in Examples 86, 87 and 88, are but so many
phases of the rapid chord-movement and accelerated modu-

---

*In Haydn's *Andante con Variazioni*, in F minor, the student will find—
beginning with measure 26 of the Finale—a slowly moving series of sixth-
chords ascending by semitones, which must have produced something of a
sensation when first performed.

EXAMPLE 88

lations instanced in Examples 82 and 84. So successful were the results above quoted, that Wagner tried similar procedures with other harmonies. Thus, in the third act of *Götterdämmerung*, when Hagen's fatal spear-thrust brings Siegfried to the earth, the Ravens of Wotan flutter across the scene accompanied by an ascending chromatic series of seventh-chords —a marvelously effective dilation of Hagen's Murder Theme. (See Section XV, Example 94b.)

Related to this illustration is the striking opening passage for strings in the final movement of Tschaikowsky's "Symphonie pathétique." In the latter instance, as the composer builds his series on the diatonic rather than the chromatic scale, a greater harmonic variety is afforded. This is particularly noticeable in the ascending flights of chords preceding each appearance of the main motive in the reprise.

EXAMPLE 89

On careful examination we shall find that these passages will admit of the closest scrutiny, as was the case with Example 84. In fact, each and every chord, if played ever so slowly, is dramatic and effective taken alone or in connection with the preceding harmony, or with what follows it. The upper $F\sharp$ in the bass clef is to be regarded as an harmonic of the lower one, and should be omitted in playing the passage on the piano.

Not long after the first production of this work in New York, Xaver Scharwenka expressed himself thus to a circle of friends: "After 'Isolde's Death,' we thought the last word in music had been uttered. Now we find in the 'Pathétique' that which is new, strikingly beautiful and deeply affecting." But certain classicists have been so highly commended for their abstention from sensuous beauty, that if a composition lay claim to melodic charm or harmonic power many good laymen at once have apprehensions lest it be lacking in intellectual qualities. Concerning Tschaikowsky's swan-song, no less a personage than Weingartner has expressed his compunctions of conscience in classifying it as a symphony. This, too, in spite of its two sonata-movements—the first and the last. However, Herr Weingartner is in good company, for in Bach's day there were excellent musicians (so says Ebenezer Prout) who declared that not one of the fugues in the Well-Tempered Clavichord was correct.

Now, harmony must either be reckoned with as a powerful factor in music, or, to use the phrase of a contemporaneous contrapuntist, it is simply a "broken reed," serving merely in a subordinate capacity. If we assume the former premise, then in passages where harmony is the important feature it should be made to evolve as symmetrically as would a purely melodic phrase in the hands of Mozart or Beethoven. In this light, the pianoforte compositions of Chopin, the music-dramas of Wagner and the symphonies of Tschaikowsky stand forth as epoch-making works.

XV

A WORLD-FORCE

The chivalrous feeling and the historic sorrow of the Pole, the easy elegance and gracefulness of the Frenchman, the romantic profundity of the German, are united in Chopin into a total of such originality that his music, though conceived for the pianoforte solely, has extended its fructifying effects beyond the sphere of that instrument. *Wilhelm Langhans,* in "History of Music."

We have seen how invaluable the rich harmonic apparatus of Chopin proved in the hands of masters capable of appreciating its subtle beauties, and the delicate differentiations of meaning imparted to a given chord-group by slight changes in the treatment of the voices. But the mere employment of complex chords and chromatic harmonies by no means implies artistic preëminence. The simple melody for horns, *unisono,* that introduces the *C*-major symphony of Schubert, possesses an appealing charm that outweighs, in merit, many entire symphonies filled to the brim with the heaviest chord-combinations. Students sometimes, in their justifiable enthusiasm for the harmonic qualities of the romantic composers, overlook the fact that some of the ablest harmonists, from Schubert to Grieg, have achieved many of their greatest triumphs by incorporating motives of varied character in their works, employing now a melodic, now a rhythmic, and again an harmonic theme.

The value of the harmonic element is indicated in direct ratio to its capacity for expressing the emotional intent of a given situation.

In literature, our sense of the fitness of things demands that simple words be employed when we deal with placid moods and the quieter emotions. On the other hand, stronger terms and more elaborate phraseology are demanded for the more impassioned outbursts of feeling and the utterances of exalted thought. An authority on rhetoric puts it: " 'The lower class' of words cannot perform the highest work. A complex feeling requires complex means of expression, and a writer who mounts into the region of ideas must use words adapted to the communication of those ideas; in short, a phraseology of more subtle significance. To see that this is so, one has only to compare a paragraph from Bunyan with one from Burke."

In the universal language of music, the analogous necessity for employing harmonies selected with nice distinction, in voicing our varied emotions, is manifest. Thus, in the treatment of childlike and naïve subjects, elemental and primitive emotions and conditions, naught is so fitting as triads—major and minor, with few inversions. More involved and intricate dramatic situations demand a more elaborate range of harmonies (chords of the seventh, ninth, etc., with their various inversions); while in the most tragic scenes the fluctuating stream of chromatic harmony, involving the element of rapid modulation, is not only justifiably employed, but positively demanded.

Manifold experience teaches us that the average intelligent layman, accustomed to Chopin, Schumann and Grieg, will find something lacking in the music of the eighteenth century. That *something* is the Harmonic Texture, which enabled the nineteenth-century masters to express to a nicety the most delicate shades of meaning.

Schumann said: "We are convinced that, were a genius like Mozart to arise in our day, he would rather write Chopinesque concertos than Mozartean ones." Richard Wagner, in discussing this subject, confessed that, were he to compose music for the thrilling scene in *Don Giovanni,* where the statue of the Commandant enters the apartment of his murderer, he would employ more striking harmonies than did Mozart.

When these great nineteenth-century masters made the above-quoted comments on the general character of the music

of such a genius as Mozart, did they imply lack of ability on
his part? By no means! They merely courageously stated
what every one ought to know, *viz.*, that in the nineteenth
century the art of music had attained a higher, fuller power
of expressiveness, especially in the department of harmony.
In the development of the grammar of harmony, Chopin
contributed most to outline the declensions of its chords, and
the conjugations of its regular and irregular modulations.
Indeed, specially significant features, rich in expressiveness,
were invented by Chopin, and subsequently adopted and elaborated by Schumann, Wagner, Grieg and others.

What I have referred to as a modulating motive is a passage, plain or figurated, as the case may be, in which an unusual harmonic progression or modulation forms a distinctive
feature. Thus, toward the end of the *A*-minor Étude, Op.
25, analyzed in Section XI, we find, as a background of the
technical figures, the deceptive cadence *A* major V_7, *C* minor
I_6. (See Example 90.) Now this is very abrupt, but *C* minor
is akin to the following chord, $D\flat$ V_7, and this, in turn, being
succeeded by *E* minor I_6, we have a sequence of *a*, at *b*.

EXAMPLE 90

The composer then proceeds at *c* as though he were about
to outline another, but breaks it into shorter members, in more
conventional sequences. The *E*-minor Concerto contains several of these modulating motives, but, as they are all highly
arpeggiated, they do not appear to be such essentially active
factors as is really the case. Later we shall encounter modulating motives, more easily recognizable as such. Example 91
shows us a beautiful outline, which occurs toward the close of
the rondo in the *E*-minor Concerto, beginning at the seven-

teenth measure after the last *tutti,* with the main theme. Observe how this outline encloses subtle inner melodies.

EXAMPLE 91

This is followed by other shorter modulating figures, with less startling features in the form of foreign material, as the object now is to establish the main key once more.

In the first movement are two remarkable illustrations of this type of modulating motive. (See Examples 92 and 93.)

EXAMPLE 92

It will be observed that in Example 92 we have to do with what is virtually a compound sequence. The motive *a a* of the first measures is continually employed in the development of the first phrase of four measures (closing with motive *b*), the second section of which is a sequence of the first two measures repeated a ninth above. We then have a free repetition of this first phrase modulating into the key of *B* major. Observe the sequential nature of the harmonic outline in measures 10 to 13, then in measures 14 to 17.

Example 93 affords still more eloquent evidence that, even at the age of nineteen, Chopin had mastered the art of harmonic development, or the development of harmonic designs. The bold chord-progressions in the opening measures (motive *a*) are followed by a sequence (measures 3 and 4). Motive *a* is then broken into one-measure members (*b b*), then into still smaller groups (*c c*). And this workmanship, as refined as it is vigorous, is overlooked and ignored, in spite of its influence on subsequent developments of the art.

EXAMPLE 93

In an article that appeared a few years ago, I devoted some space to the discussion of such thematic material; among the illustrations given were the theme in Chopin's Fantaisie Op. 49, measures 21 to 28 (repeated),* and the second part of

---

*Another beautiful specimen may be found in measures 101 to 109 of the same work.

the Pilgrims' Chorus from *Tannhäuser,* together with numerous excerpts from Wagner's later works. I must repeat
just enough of what I said, at that time, to touch on the fact
that, in Wagner's hands, harmony had become so powerful a
factor in giving the fine discriminating shades of meaning to
a bit of dialogue, or the subtle changes of mood which come
over the speaker, that not infrequently, with a few chords
devoid of rhythm or melody (save the most rudimentary),
we have the gist of the matter at once.   Brünnhilde greets
Siegmund with her Death-Message; Hagen plots Siegfried's
death, or gives him the Draught of Forgetfulness.   (See
respectively motives *a, b* and *c,* in Example 94.)

EXAMPLE 94

It seems singular that, in spite of the great popularity of
the Wagnerian music-dramas, so few should appreciate the
nature and value of these harmonic designs.   The majority
seem to consider the upper voice of these motives the main
feature, as would be the case with a theme of Mozart or Beethoven.   An able pianist and teacher in Berlin, in speaking of
the Fate Theme (Example 94a), told his pupil that, in this
instance, Wagner had employed an *Ur-Motiv,* that is, a
traditional theme used by others; among them Beethoven in
the second movement of his sonata, Op. 81.   If the reader
will but take the trouble to play the first measure of this
movement, and compare it with the Wagner motive, he will
find it to be a melodic figure, well harmonized; but, while the
outline is like that of Wagner, the latter is unquestionably an
harmonic design.

Again, in all thematic catalogues of the Wagnerian music-dramas, from Hans von Wolzogen's "Leitfaden" down to the text-book of the Nibelungen trilogy recently issued by Schott, the harmonic themes are frequently indicated by the upper voice only,* or perchance, two may be given. Even when we have four upper voices of a complex harmonic theme (as in the case of the Wanderer Motive), the result is comically incomplete. Of course, it is more convenient, but, for the sake of accuracy, a little more pains ought to be bestowed on the matter. These illustrations serve to show that there is much to learn in following out the fine points in the art of the great harmonists, Chopin, Wagner, Grieg and Tschaikowsky. Furthermore, there is also much to be learned concerning their logical development.

Of course, all motives, whether melodic or harmonic, do not lend themselves to the processes of development with equal readiness. This axiom is brought home to one early in life. While still a boy, long before I had heard an orchestra, I noted in my sketch-book a theme which at once interested and baffled me. I afterward found it to be practically identical with the opening measures of Liszt's *A*-major Concerto. (See Example 95, a and b.)

EXAMPLE 95

With the return to the tonic key, in the third measure, the impetus dies, and there seems to be no incentive to further progress. Even Liszt, in treating this modulating motive,

---

*Curiously enough, Wagner himself, in a letter to Frau Wesendonck, referring to the longing for Nirvana, quotes the *melodic* portion only of the opening theme of the *Vorspiel* to *Tristan und Isolde*.

fails to give it such plastic elaborations as he did in treating the motive of the $E\flat$-major Concerto (likewise a modulating motive). In the former case the development consists merely in repetitions of the motive, with new pianistic figures that continually grow in interest and difficulty; in the latter instance there is a constant organic growth. Liszt employs new and unusual means of extending and abbreviating, in a manner thoroughly homogeneous, the original design, and this, too, in a style of instrumentation wholly his own. It will be seen that the motto of the $E\flat$ Concerto offers a greater variety of members, or germs, for development or expansion than does the theme from the Concerto in A. This obviously facilitates matters. (See Examples 96, a, b, c and d.)

EXAMPLE 96

In one of my early works I experimented with a modulating motive of a nature akin to Example 95. One day I showed it to an elderly New York colleague, an erudite and able theorist who, during his lifetime, was regarded by some as the best fugue teacher in the city. He advised me to begin more simply and demonstrated how, by taking the upper voice alone at first, it might be treated in canon-form, in contrary motion, in the inversion, etc. That the character of the motive lay wholly in the harmonic progressions, was something he failed to perceive.

Richard Strauss attributes the richness of texture in Wagner's music to "the broader line treatment, such as we find in the Bach fugues and the later quartets of Beethoven."* A

---

*Cf. Strauss-Berlioz, "Orchestration."

glance at the works in question will indeed reveal the free line treatment, that is, we see figures running in opposite directions, colliding or intersecting in such a way as to produce cross-relations and unresolved dissonances, justifiable by virtue of the preservation of the outlines involved; such we often find in Wagner and sometimes in Chopin. (See the *A*-minor Étude Op. 25, already quoted.)

Let us listen carefully to the wonderful harmonic designs given in Example 94. They reveal in a most mysterious, but none the less emphatic, and singularly suggestive manner, the moods of the actors in the great Norse drama. In studying the scoring of these passages, do we find "the broader line treatment" of Bach and the later Beethoven? No! nothing of the kind, nor could the criss-crossings of any number of lines produce the emotional effects here brought forth. In the subsequent development of even this complex material, Wagner has indeed employed multifold contrapuntal devices. Nevertheless, here we deal with a most original method of creating a mood, in which two elements are predominant—harmony and orchestration. No one had ever conceived such a method before, and this high degree of excellence has since been approached but rarely.

To what influences do we attribute such unusual phenomena? Chopin and Berlioz. Incidentally be it remarked that neither of these masters were Germans; unless we employ the term in its very broadest meaning, implying descendants of the Teutonic peoples of Middle Europe, colored by the Slavic elements on the East and by the Celtic on the West.

There seems to be an obsession, not only in Germany but elsewhere, that unless a composer holds exclusively to German models, he is lost. In justification of this view it may be urged that, as are the poets of Greece and Rome to the world's literature, so are the composers of Germany's classical period to the literature of music—inevitable and indispensable. But we must not overlook the fact that when Dante, Chaucer and

other poets emancipated themselves from the yoke of obsoles-
cent languages, and elected to express their ideas in their
mother-tongues, they added, to their classical training,
knowledge of subjects nearer at hand. Although they
frequently lead the old mythological *dramatis personæ* across
the stage, they also acquaint us with new and vigorous char-
acters indigenous to the soil of their respective countries. The
truly independent musician supplements his German educa-
tion with all that enables him to express his own individuality.
Thus, Wagner, having early devoted himself to Italian
models, retained such features as were helpful, discarded the
rest, and in searching for stimulating and dramatic elements
took the best of everything wherever he could find it, whether
within the boundaries of Germany or elsewhere.

How much more suggestive of universality would our
world-language—music—become if it were regarded as one
to which various peoples have contributed! Were the claim
broadly stated, that we derive our melody from Italy; our
harmony from Germany; rhythm from the Slavs and Mag-
yars, and orchestral color from the French, we should have a
proposition decidedly more poetic and plausible than when
we attribute all factors to one country or one people.

Both Chopin and Wagner were indebted to Beethoven for
their knowledge of the science of thematic development, but
the former was the first to apply and adapt it to the requirements of the new harmonic material. It will thus be seen that
Wagner was doubly indebted to Chopin, and his kinship to
the Polish master is as evident as his relationship to Beethoven.* The illustrations that have been given in evidence

---

*Wagner laid stress on conducting without the score. I have seen in the
library of Mr. Karl Klinkerfuss, at Stuttgart, Beethoven's Fifth Symphony
in the handwriting of Wagner, who made the copy merely as an exercise in
memorizing. The fact that he conducted Chopin's E-minor Concerto in one
of the London Philharmonic concerts proves his thorough familiarity with
that work and the principles embodied therein. This in and by itself testifies
to Chopin's influence at first hand.

of this are not to be regarded in the light of plagiarisms, as the reminiscence-hunter loves to put it, but as showing how Wagner grasped the situation, investigated and applied the principles underlying Chopin's system of architecture, and in many instances boldly amplified them. It will thus appear to those who can view the question without bias or prejudice, that, by virtue of his rare mentality, nourished from various sources under such peculiar conditions, Chopin manifested traits not alone Polish, but French, German, Italian and even Oriental, thus enabling him, in a certain sense, to speak a more universal tone-language than Bach or Beethoven. He may not have treated such a variety of topics, and his means of expression was restricted practically to one instrument, but his language was more highly inflected, and his vocabulary more extensive.

No one since Michael Angelo has surpassed Richard Wagner in all-comprehensiveness. But we know from what he himself has said, that his universality was acquired through patient, indefatigable study of the greatest masters; and when we listen to his music, with its sonorous dispersion, its ever-moving deceptive cadences, its rich harmonies, logically elaborated, we feel instinctively that among the most potent forces which shaped the remarkable career of the Master of Bayreuth, must be mentioned the art and science of Frédéric Chopin.

CODA

Those men of genius who cannot be surpassed may be equalled.
How? By being different. *Victor Hugo.*

In reviewing the masterpieces illustrating the essential characteristics of Chopin's art, I find that, in spite of all efforts to avoid expressions of opinion concerning the quality of these works, such expressions have nevertheless obtruded themselves. In extenuation be it said, that Chopin's architectural designs, like those of Bach, Beethoven and Wagner, often exert a direct influence upon the character of the material itself. Therefore, in giving voice to one's admiration of the specifically architectural features of a given composition, one unavoidably extends the application of this commendation to the subject-matter, and even to the spirit of the music itself.

Highly as I admire the unrivalled beauty of his pianoforte compositions, I am even more fascinated by the mastery displayed in the workmanship, but most of all do I revere his conscientiousness in maintaining an exalted ideal which has exerted a beneficent influence on the art of music in general.

In order to accentuate the reminiscent character of this coda, I have again quoted the Gallic epigram from Victor Hugo's remarkable essay on Shakespeare. To this I should like to add, by way of filling in the interstices, the Teutonic moralizing of Max Müller, who, in dealing with the same fundamental idea, says:

"It is in the nature of things that every new generation of scholars should perfect their tools and with these discover flaws in the work left by their predecessors. . . . If the Cyclopean stones of the Pelasgeans are not like the finished works of art by Phidias, what would the Parthenon be without the walls ascribed to the Cyclops? It is the same in all sciences; and we must try to be just, both to the genius of those who created, and to those who polished and refined."

INDEX OF NAMES, ETC.

Æolian mode, 15; used by Chopin, 17.

Amati, 144.

Amazon, brilliancy of forests, 63.

American negro minstrel clog-dancing, 22.

Ancien régime, music of, 1.

Anglo-Saxons, music, 64.

Antiphonal work, 121.

Arabs, music on Midway Plaisance, 16; their scales, etc., 20, 21; the Zamir, a form of aulos or oboe, 132.

Architectural methods of Greek and Gothic builders compared, 129.

Architecture, Egyptian, 46; Grecian, 46, 129; Roman, 129; Romanesque, 120; Norman, 27; (Gothic)— Early English, 27; Decorated Gothic, 27; Perpendicular Gothic, 27; Flamboyant Gothic, 120.

Arts, the moving, 80; the static, 80.

Aulos virtuosos and their descriptive music, 132.

Bach, J. S., 2, 3, 12, 13, 25, 27, 35, 45, 52, 59, 66, 81, 82, 91, 106; thematic development, 127; expansiveness of themes, 128; 132, 134; free part-leading, 136; long series of sequences, 138; 146, 179.

Barcarolle, highly idealized Rondo, 90.

Bavarian Schuhplättler, 22.

Beethoven, L. van, 4, 10, 11, 12, 13, 25, 26, 35, 39; his virtuosity, 45; emphasis of primary chords, 47; his sketch-books, 59; 64, 66, 75, 76, 84, 86, 91, 93, 94, 99, 106, 117, 119; Heroic Symphony, 122; economy of material, 126; thematic development, 127; 134, 135; independent part-leading, 136;

Beethoven, L. van—*Continued* thematic cadenzas, 140, 141; extends compass of strings, 144; inadequacy of natural horns and trumpets to the expression of his ideas, 147 to 150; 152; harmonic material compared with that of C., 160, 167; the later quartettes, 175, 176; C. and Wagner indebted to Beethoven for science of thematic development, 177; 179.

Bel canto, C.'s admiration of, 24.

Bellini, Vincenzo, C.'s attachment to, 24, 133.

Berlioz, Hector, 2, 37, 45; influence on Bizet, 91; 145, 151; influence on Wagner, 176.

Bizet, Georges, influence of C. shown in respect to refined harmonies, 91; application of C.'s freer song- and rondo-forms, 91; his return to main key vague and poetic, 92; Quintette in *Carmen* a specimen of C.'s "revitalized" rondo, 92; semblance of remoteness between closely related harmonies, 104; 119, 137, 138.

Böhm, Theobald, 145, 157.

Brahms, Johannes, 8, 114.

Bülow, Hans von, 52, 93, 100, 134.

Bunyan, John, his simple phraseology, 169.

Burke, Edmund, literary style, 169.

Cadenza, vocal, 133; instrumental, 133, 140, 141; æsthetic value of, 141, 142; thematic, 140, 141.

California, abandoned mines, 106.

Cantus firmus, 8.

Catholic, original import of term, 158.

Chamber works of C., 111, 153.

Chaucer, Geoffrey, expressed himself with greater ease in poetry than in prose, 80; "Triple Roundel" quoted, 81; like Dante, added to classical themes others of local interest, 176, 177.

Chinese, ancient, aware of relationship of tonic and dominant, 83.

Chopin, one of the 1810 group, 2; value of the study of his structural innovations, 4; intellectual qualities overlooked, 5 and 6; misleading statements concerning his architectural art, 6, 7 and 8; C. a great Bach student, 9, 27, 28 and 29; apprehends relationship between remote keys, 13; Wagner's estimate of C., 46; principles applied, 97, 100, 101, 102; ability to give closely related keys a semblance of remoteness, 13, 103; his system applied by Bizet, 104; his use of Polish national airs, 14 *et seq.;* application of mediæval modes, 15 to 19; Oriental elements in his music, 20; Parisian influence on C. salutary, 21; C.'s music shows harmonic distinction from the beginning, 22; admiration for Bellini manifest in his diatonic melodies, 24, 133; stimulus afforded by improved pianoforte, 25, 26 and 27; allusion to Bach in Majorca letter, 28; mechanical device for stretching fingers, 28; great care in chord-distribution, 29; bewildering harmonies often merely decorations of simple material, 30, 31, 32; ideal treatment of virtuoso passages, 39 *et seq.;* difference between his style and that of Beethoven, 40, 41; unusual modulatory schemes involving deceptive cadences, 48, 102; unique achievements with simple diatonic scale, 41, 42; C.'s treatment of lyric forms as compared with the German, 64, 65, 68, 71; unusual combination of lyric elements, 73 to 78; new methods of treating rondo, 86 to 91; the Fantaisie in F minor a highly complex rondo, 91; variety of keys and cadences employed by C. in the smaller forms, 96 to 103; mastery of the sonata elements, 109 to 117; the-

matic character of his music not appreciated by Scholtz, 120; remarkable structural ingenuity displayed in great *A*-minor Étude, 122 to 126; *F*-minor Étude, Op. 10, shows Beethoven-like gift of creating much out of little, 127; his themes as compact and expansive as those of the Bach inventions, 128; C.'s masterly solution of romantic harmonic problems, 130; C.'s tendency to beautify and decorate, 131; decorated counterpoint, 136; decorated organ-point, 137; reiterated figures, 137, 138; decorated sequences, 138; thematic cadenzas, 140; the improved pianoforte as a stimulus to the imagination, 144; the orchestra had not attained a parallel perfection, 144; the classical orchestra inadequate to the execution of C.'s harmonic themes, 150; such themata unavailable for full orchestra till Wagner introduced chromatic horns and trumpets, 151; C.'s efforts to increase expressiveness of orchestra, 156; suggests various original effects, 156, 157; shows traits universal as well as national, 158 *et seq.;* C.'s rich harmonic vocabulary, 169; invents modulating motive, 170; the harmonic design, 172, 173; difference between harmonic design and melodic theme, 173 to 176; Wagner and others indebted to C. for the art of developing *harmonic themes,* 177; *Concerto in E minor* conducted by Wagner, 177; C.'s harmonic language more highly inflected than that of the classical masters, 178; 179.

Chopin, Prof. Nicolas, father of the composer, 10.

Clavichord, its thin tone, 132.

Climate, influence upon art, 46.

Clog-dancing, 22.

Composers, young, need of training other than classical, 13.

Copernicus, Nicolaus, 3.

Cossack horsemen, chanting of, 66, 67.

Cristofori, Bartolommeo, inventor of pianoforte, 25.

INDEX OF COMPOSITIONS